How to
Embroider Texture and Pattern

How to Embroider Texture and Pattern

Landauer Publishing, www.landauerpub.com, is an imprint of Fox Chapel Publishing Company, Inc.

Project Team
Managing Editor: Gretchen Bacon
Acquisitions Editor: Amelia Johanson
Editor: Christa Oestreich
Designers: Wendy Reynolds, Michael Douglas
Photographer: Melissa Galbraith
Proofreader: Jeremy Hauck
Indexer: Jay Kreider

Shutterstock used: Flaffy (yellow flowers: front cover, 6, 158, back cover);
K.Decor (eucalyptus leaves: front cover, 5, 158, back cover).

ISBN 978-1-63981-021-5

Library of Congress Control Number: 2023932908

We are always looking for talented authors. To submit an idea, please send a brief inquiry to acquisitions@foxchapelpublishing.com.

Note to Professional Copy Services:
The publisher grants you permission to make up to six copies of any quilt patterns in this book for any customer who purchased this book and states the copies are for personal use.

Printed in China
Second printing

How to
Embroider Texture and Pattern

20 Designs that Celebrate Pattern, Color, and Pop-Up Stitching

MELISSA GALBRAITH

Landauer Publishing

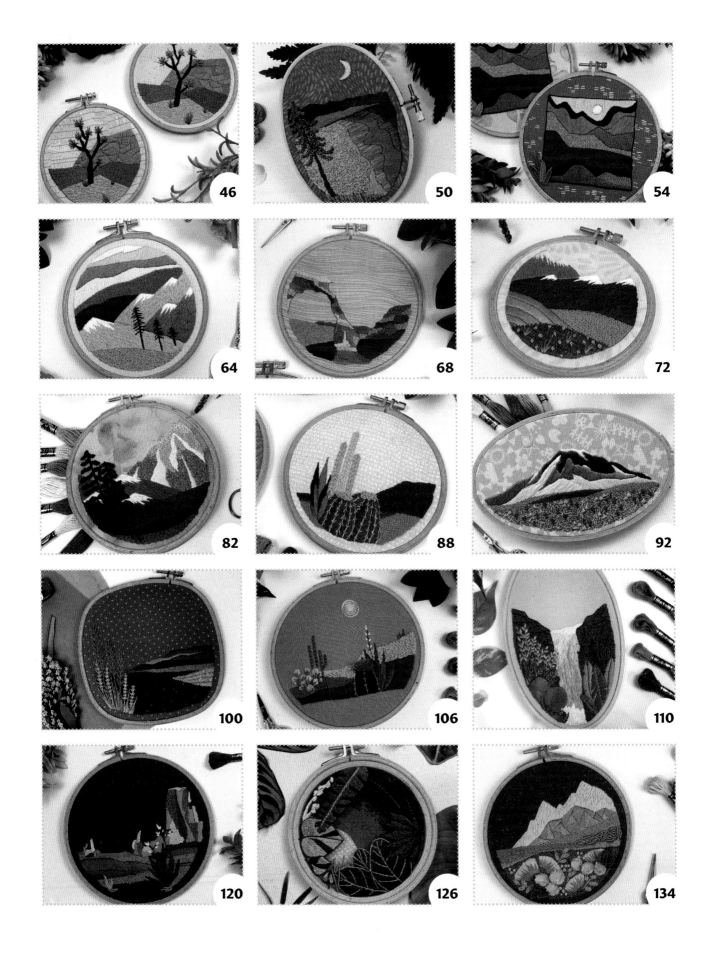

46

50

54

64

68

72

82

88

92

100

106

110

120

126

134

60

76

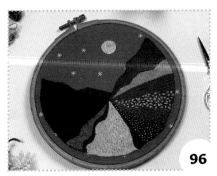

96

116

140

Contents

Introduction 6

Materials Prep 8

  Fabric 8

  Hoops 9

  Transferring the Pattern 11

  Thread Prep 13

  Scissors 15

  Needles 15

  Knots 17

Stitch Glossary 20

PROJECTS

  Joshua Tree 46

  Where the Forest Meets the Beach 50

  Mojave Hues 54

  Hidden Beach Cove 60

  Mountains at Sunset 64

  Desert Arches 68

  Purple Mountains Majesty 72

  A Walk Among the Wildflowers 76

  Scenic Lookout 82

  Desert Oasis 88

  A Pacific Northwest Spring 92

  Mountain Brook 96

  From the Heartland 100

  It Was All a Mirage 106

  Tropical Waterfall 110

  A Walk Along the English Seaside 116

  Valley Views 120

  Cenote Plunge 126

  Flower Field Mountains 134

  Forest Foraging 140

How to Finish Your Embroidery in the Hoop 146

Patterns 148

About Melissa 158

Index 159

Introduction

When creating the patterns for the book, I pulled inspiration from the travels my family and I have taken across the globe as well as from my bucket list. You'll see deserts from California and Arizona, the Rocky Mountains in Montana and Washington, tropical waterfalls from Kauai, and much more. To properly capture the feeling of those places, ordinary stitching would not do. There is so much life in a waterfall or rock formation, so playing with thread and stitches makes them feel much more real. But what truly makes these pieces stand apart are the fabrics I use as backgrounds. Wavy lines simulate hot air, while dots on a dark fabric represent a night sky; each scene can display a completely different mood depending on what fabric you choose. A bold print can be just another element to make your piece shine. I'll show you how to achieve a special piece you'll want to keep on display or gift to someone you love!

My mom is the craftiest person I know, and she taught me the joy of making things by hand. My sisters and I had the opportunity to try everything from sewing and bobbin lace to hand embroidery and papier-mâché. Funny story, when I first told my mom I was getting back into embroidery, she said, "You hated that as a kid!" While I'm almost positive my elementary school self was a terrible embroidery student, I am forever grateful for my mother's patience and willingness to share these skills with me. After graduating college and getting into the workforce, I found myself constantly behind a computer and in need of a portable, mindful, tactile craft. After trying a few other things, I stumbled back into hand embroidery and the rest is history—well, actually, it's MCreativeJ, my small business where I now teach my fellow makers the joys of stitching and creating by hand.

I call myself a landscape lover. When I got back into embroidery as an adult, I dabbled in many different embroidery styles until finding one that felt like me. Pulling from nature and my surroundings has felt like the most organic and natural way to create embroidery designs; in fact, I can often be seen walking around my neighborhood taking photos on my phone to reference for future patterns. This love of nature and the textures that surround us inspired me to create an embroidery book focusing on the landscapes that inspire me. I hope you enjoy creating these textural landscapes and find inspiration in your own surroundings.

Happy stitching!
—Melissa

Materials Prep

Ready to get started? This section will walk you through necessary materials like fabric, hoops, thread, and needles, as well as cover the basics of pattern transfers, splitting thread, knots, and more. Even if you've embroidered before, you're sure to find helpful tips for a good foundation.

Fabric

One of the many great things about embroidery is that you can stitch on anything. I mean it! I've stitched on some interesting materials (tulle, scuba gear, stretchy cosplay material, and sweaters, just to name a few) and seen fellow embroidery artists stitch on rackets, colanders, cars, and fences. You name it, it can probably be stitched on.

If you're new to embroidery, that might seem a little intimidating, so let's start with the basics. I often find that using a fabric that has minimal stretch is a good starting point when learning to embroider. Fabrics like **quilting cotton or linen** are great options. As you build up your embroidery expertise, don't be afraid to explore other fabrics.

EXPLORE COLOR AND PATTERN

Over the last few decades, embroidery has been stitched primarily on solid, often white, fabric. I know you've seen embroidered pillowcases and bed linens. My first embroidery was on one of those white preprinted pillowcases! As we take a modern approach to embroidery, I want you to explore color and pattern!

One of my favorite parts of creating a design is choosing the thread and fabric. I love to think about how a pattern material could add motion, emotion, or extra dimension to a design:

- Could spots on the fabric make it seem like there are clouds in the sky?
- Would a floral pattern fabric add an extra layer of dimension to your landscape?
- Would chevrons or other lines create the effect of additional mountains or air flowing by?
- Does the background fabric complement or contrast with the thread colors?

Let your imagination run wild!

Each pattern in this book lists which fabric the sample is stitched on, but I encourage you to explore different pattern fabrics as you choose your own materials for these projects.

Clockwise (from top left): Transfer paper, print fabric, oval hoop, a variety of thread skeins, two circular hoops, thread gloss, pins, erasable pen, embroidery needle, and embroidery scissors.

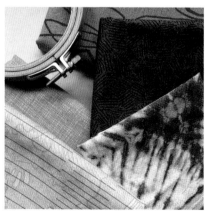

Colors and prints can add a new layer of interest to your piece. Check your local craft store for inspiration!

Hoops

To keep the fabric taut when stitching, it's important to have your embroidery in an embroidery hoop. These come in all sorts of sizes, shapes (circles, ovals, squares, and triangles), and materials (bamboo, beechwood, metal, and plastic). Every stitcher has their own preference. I love Nurge beechwood hoops. I find these thick, high-quality, screw-top hoops to make embroidery a joy.

No matter what type of embroidery hoop you use, the important feature to look for is that the inner and outer rings of the hoop fit together nicely. If the two rings have gaps or pull away from each other when tightened in the hoop, the tension of the fabric is thrown off. Gaps between the inner and outer rings tend to make the fabric gape and pull awkwardly, making embroidery less enjoyable.

In this book, each pattern details the size and type of embroidery hoop I used to create the pattern. These are just recommendations, and I encourage you to find what type of hoop you like best.

Think about how the size and shape of a hoop would add to your finished piece. You might be surprised with your choices, once you experiment!

PLACING FABRIC IN THE HOOP

1 **Cut the fabric to size.** Start by laying out the fabric on a flat surface. Place the embroidery hoop on top of the fabric. Using fabric scissors, cut an inch away from the hoop's edge. Remove the extra fabric.

2 **Unscrew the embroidery hoop enough so that the inner ring easily pops out of the outer ring.** Place the inner ring flat on the table, then lay the fabric on top of it. Press the outer ring onto the fabric and inner ring, sandwiching the three pieces together.

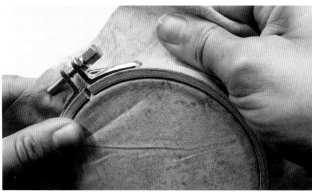

3 **Tighten the hoop around the fabric.** Gently tighten the top screw. While doing so, tug the fabric along the edges so that it starts to get taut in the hoop. Continue to tighten the top screw and gently tug the fabric. The fabric in the hoop will be ready to embroider when it sounds like a drum when tapped.

Transferring the Pattern

This part of the embroidery process can feel daunting, especially if you don't feel like you have strong drawing skills. The great thing about embroidery is that there are different ways to transfer your design onto your fabric. Here's two of the methods I like to use.

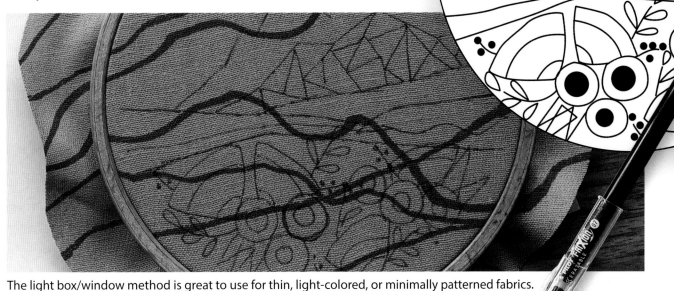

The light box/window method is great to use for thin, light-colored, or minimally patterned fabrics.

LIGHT BOX/WINDOW

This transfer method is easy and great for sunny days. As someone who lives in the Pacific Northwest, I see a lot of dreary, rainy days, so a **light box** also comes in handy and does the same thing.

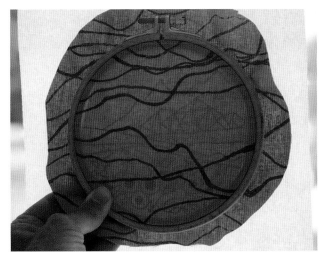

1 **Print or trace your design to size.** If you're tracing, use a dark pen to clearly see your lines.

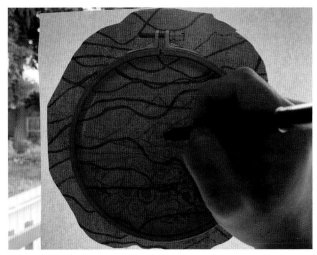

2 **Tape the sketch to a well-lit window or a light box.** With your fabric stretched in the hoop, place it over the pattern and transfer the design using an **erasable pen** (I use Pilot FriXion erasable pens). Don't worry if you don't get your lines quite right; this pen is heat erasable, so you can easily start again.

TRANSFER PAPER

I'm a fan of transfer paper because it's almost like creating a water-soluble sticker for your fabric.

1 **Decide if you're going to print or trace your design.** You can print directly onto a **water-soluble transfer paper** (I use Sulky Fabri-Solvy). For this example, I've printed my design on printer paper and will trace onto the water-soluble transfer paper. Use a pencil so the ink doesn't run into your design later.

2 **Finish tracing the design.** Trim the transfer paper to ¼" (6mm) around the edge of the design.

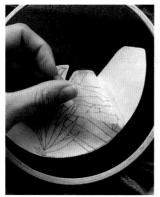 

3 **Peel off the backing.** Place the design, sticky side down, onto fabric stretched in a hoop.

4 **When you're done stitching, simply remove your embroidery from the hoop.** Wash the template away by soaking in warm water, then let your embroidery air dry. It's important not to scrunch or wrinkle your embroidery when rinsing the transfer paper, otherwise it can distort your finished embroidery. Nobody wants all their hard work to go to waste!

This transfer method is great if you're working with thick or dark fabrics, fabrics with bold patterns, and clothing. It acts as a stabilizer, too!

Tip

One of the drawbacks of this transfer method is that the transfer paper can make your needle sticky or gummy when stitching. To avoid this, just rinse and dry your needle occasionally.

Thread Prep

For projects in this book, you'll use **6-strand DMC® embroidery thread**. This means each skein of thread includes six individual strands. Each pattern details which color to use and how many strands of thread to use in that portion of the pattern.

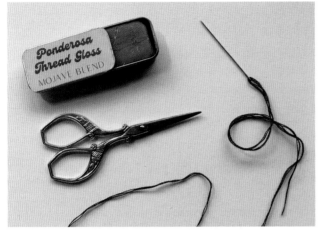

Clockwise (starting top left): Thread gloss, an embroidery needle threaded with three strands of embroidery floss, and embroidery scissors.

There is a variety of floss types out there, but I encourage beginners to start with the colors I've supplied. Once you're comfortable, then you can experiment!

CUTTING THE THREAD

Those new to embroidery might not realize that cutting the right length of thread makes a big difference! Thread that is too long can get tangled, but having a length that is too short means you'll be constantly threading your needle. Here's a good method for solving that issue.

1 **To get started, I flip the skein of thread so that the numbers are at the top.** Find the tail end of thread sticking out of the skein top.

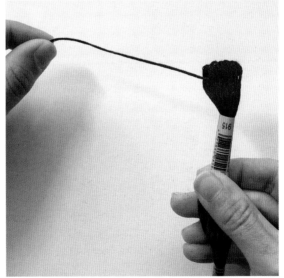

2 **Hold the skein by your nose and pull out one arm's length of thread.** This will give you a consistent measurement without using a ruler or measuring tape.

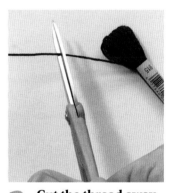

3 **Cut the thread away from the skein.** This measurement will be different for everyone. It's the right amount of thread to ensure that the thread is less likely to get tangled. You can always cut the thread a shorter length, but I do not recommend anything longer.

SPLITTING THE THREAD

Many of the projects in this book use a variety of thread weights. Varying the thread weights (1 strand, 3 strands, or even 6 strands) allows you to create different textures and details.

1 To split the thread apart, pinch the thread between your fingers at one end. Notice there are six strands.

2 Gently pull one strand away from the bunch. Pull straight up and not apart. The thread should bunch under your fingers.

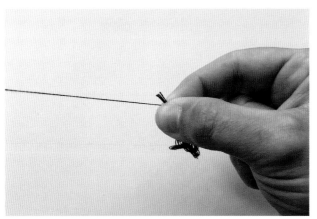

3 After the one strand is away from the bunch, lay it flat on the table. Flatten out the thread it was pulled from.

4 Repeat the process until you have the desired number of strands. Do not try to pull more than one strand of thread from the bunch at a time. Pulling out multiple strands at a time usually results in a tangled knotted mess.

Tip

Along with different thread weights, you can also create your own color variations by combining strands from different threads. I've found variegated thread colors to be harder to find and much more expensive than standard cotton embroidery thread. Combining strands from different colors is a simple and inexpensive way to create your own variegated thread options.

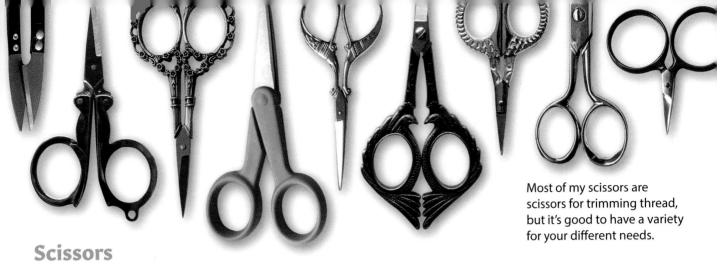

Most of my scissors are scissors for trimming thread, but it's good to have a variety for your different needs.

Scissors

You might have noticed I own a lot of scissors. I love collecting colorful and unique scissor designs. There are so many out there! To embroider, you really only need two types of scissors.

The first is a **large, sharp pair of scissors** to cut fabric. I've found that larger scissors make it easier to cut fabric in straight, even lines. In my studio, I have scissors labeled for fabric and paper. This is because fabric scissors should only be used for fabric. Using them on other materials will dull the blades, making them harder to use and your fabric fray after cutting.

The second is a **small, sharp pair of scissors** to trim threads. Smaller scissors make it easier to trim thread close to the hoop back and get into small spaces, like near the hoop edge. I recommend finding a pair that fits easily in your fingers and has a longer scissor blade.

In addition to smaller scissors, you can find **curved scissors**, which have a slightly bowed tip. These can make it easier to cut threads close to the fabric. **Thread snips** are another good option for cutting thread. These are often spring-loaded blades that, when pressed together, can trim thread.

Needles

Needles for hand sewing come in all thicknesses and lengths. If you're new to embroidery, I recommend trying a variety pack of embroidery needles to help you find what thickness and length of needle you prefer.

It's important in embroidery that the needle doesn't damage the fabric as you stitch. If the needle is creating holes or causing distortions in the fabric, it's probably too thick of a needle to be using for that fabric. In general, thinner, delicate fabrics use thinner, delicate needles. Thicker, heavier fabrics use longer, thicker needles.

When I embroider, I usually prefer to use a **#5 embroidery needle.** These are medium-weight embroidery needles that are about 1½" (3.8cm) in length. I like the #5 needle because it works with most fabrics, it can handle 1–6 strands of thread, and the length feels comfortable in my fingers. They make needles of all sorts of lengths and thicknesses,

and you can use any needle you'd like. The important thing is to find one you like, that the needle is easy to thread, and it doesn't damage the fabric when used.

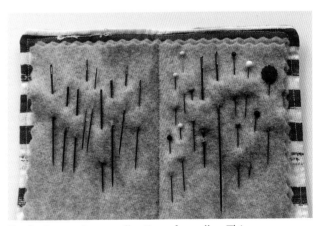

I've built up a large collection of needles. This needlebook is a great way to store needles and pins as well as make it easy for me to find the right one!

THREADING THE NEEDLE

This can often be the trickiest part of embroidery! Here are a few tips to make it easier. And if all else fails, use a needle threader.

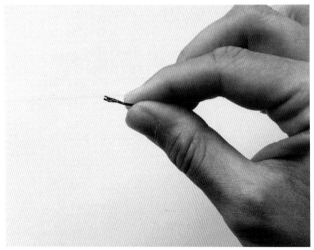

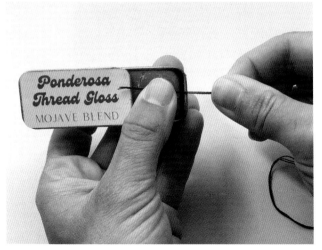

1 **After you've split apart the thread (page 14), align all the strands you want to use.** Make sure that the end being threaded through the needle is even. If the thread is frizzy or uneven, trim the edge.

2 **Use thread gloss or get the thread wet so that the strands stick together.** When I first started embroidering, I put the thread ends into my mouth to get them wet and to stick together. Now, I like to use **thread gloss**. This is a scented beeswax mix that acts as a conditioner for the thread. Not only does it help the thread stick together, but it also helps the thread from tangling. And it's easy to use. Simply run the thread across the wax.

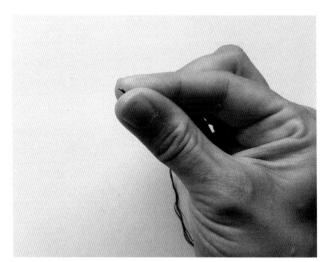

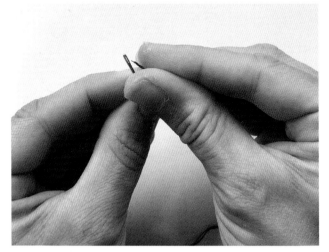

3 **When you're ready to thread the needle, flatten the thread into a straight line.** This will make it easier to fit as you pass the thread through the eye of the needle.

4 **Hold as close as you can to the end of the thread length.** This will help you guide the thread into the eye of the needle without the thread bending or splitting apart.

Knots

Knots are important for starting and ending a thread when embroidering. This section will cover how to knot the end of your thread to start stitching and how to finish the thread on the back of your embroidery with a knot.

You might notice there are also knots listed in the Stitch Glossary (page 20). These knots, like the French knot or Danish knot, are textural knots that sit on the front of the fabric. The knots detailed in this section will be on the back of the embroidery.

KNOTTING THE END OF THE THREAD

I like to use the **quilter's knot** when knotting the end of my thread. This gives you a solid knot all in one.

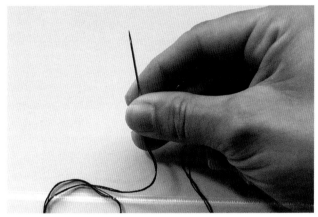

1 **Make sure the needle is threaded and one side is slightly shorter than the other.**

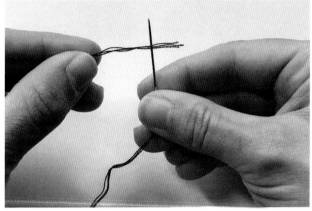

2 **Hold the needle pointy side up in your dominant hand.** Pinch the very end of the long end of thread in your other hand and cross it in front of the needle, creating a *T* shape with the needle and thread end.

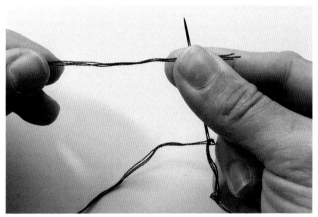

3 **Pinch where the thread and needle cross together between the thumb and finger that's holding the needle.** In your nondominant hand, pinch the loop of thread about 3"–4" (7.5–10cm) away from where the thread and needle are held together.

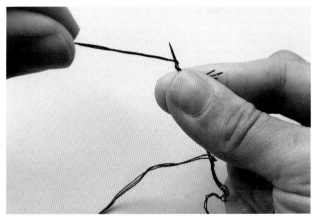

4 **Taking the top part of that loop, wrap it around the top of the needle three times.** Tug the thread so it's tightly wrapped.

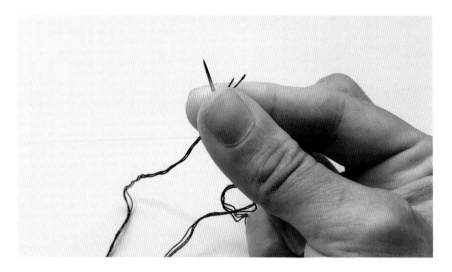

5 **Pinch the wrapped thread between the thumb and finger that is holding the needle.** Let go of the loop of thread in your other hand.

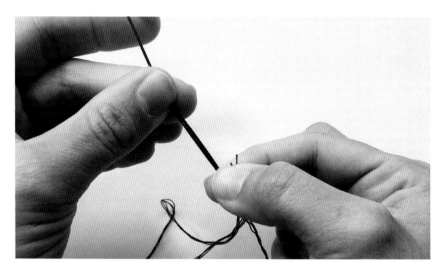

6 **Continue pinching the wrapped thread as you pull the needle straight up.** Grab the needle at the eye as you pull so that it doesn't come unthreaded.

7 **Keep pinching the thread wrap until you get to the end of the thread.** This will create a knot. I usually trim the end of the thread after the knot to ½" (1.3cm).

KNOTTING THE THREAD ON THE EMBROIDERY BACK

I like to use a **slip knot** when ending my thread on the back of an embroidery. To do this, you'll want to have at least 3" (7.5cm) of thread to work with.

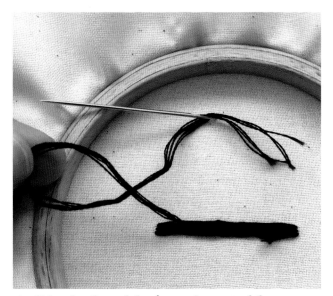

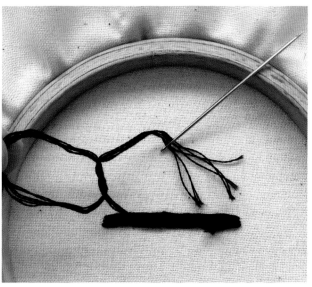

1 Take the thread that's coming out of the embroidery and make a loop.

2 Bring the needle through the loop of thread. Where everything crosses is going to be the knot. Use your fingers to work the crossed portion of the loop down to the back of the fabric.

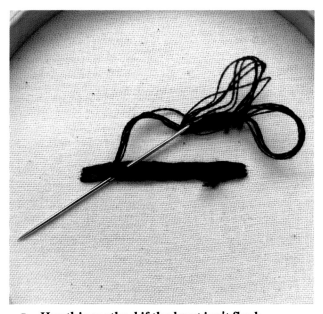

3 Create a knot. When it's flush with the back of the fabric, gently tug the thread end. Cut away the extra thread.

4 Use this method if the knot isn't flush with the fabric. Run your threaded needle underneath some of the stitches on the back of the embroidery. This will tug the thread and knot down to the back and protect it from coming undone. Then cut away the thread.

Stitch Glossary

This section covers all 33 embroidery stitches used in this book. Each stitch creates a unique texture with some being similar to or variations of others. I hope you enjoy giving them a try and creating textural designs.

BACK STITCH

The back stitch creates short stitches in a row. Like the name suggests, this stitch is made by leaving a space and then going back to fill it in. When the back stitch is used to fill an area, rows are offset like a brick wall.

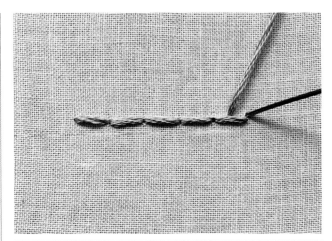

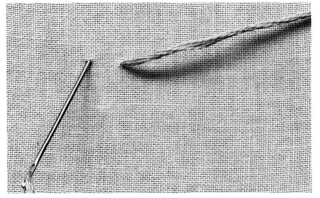

1 **Bring the needle up from the back of the fabric about ⅛"–¼"** (3-6mm) **away from the start of the row.** Then bring the needle back down through the fabric where the stitch will end. This creates a single back stitch.

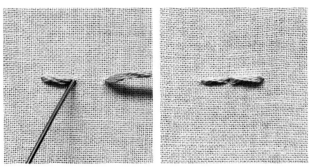

2 **Add another back stitch to the row.** Leave a space along the row and bring the needle up through the fabric. To connect this back stitch to the last, bring the needle back down through the fabric in the hole of the last stitch.

3 **To create the "brick wall" texture, offset each row of back stitches.** Bring the needle up one row above the line of stitches you made. Insert the needle at the middle of the stitch below, then back stitch to the end of the row. Bring the needle up from the back at the middle of the next stitch. Stitch through the first hole in the row. Repeat for a solid texture.

BULLION KNOT

The bullion knot is a long, cylindrical knot. This knot can be used to add a slightly raised texture to a design for leaves, ground texture, and even as flowers.

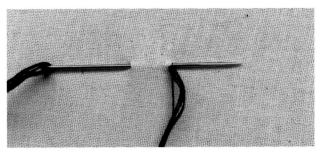

1 Bring the needle up from the back of the fabric to the front. Choose the length of the bullion knot you wish to create and bring the needle back down through the fabric. Before pushing the needle all the way through the fabric, bring it back up next to where the thread is coming out of the fabric.

2 With the needle in the fabric, wrap the thread around the needle. The length of the wraps should be similar to the size of the space left in the fabric. The thread should be tightly wrapped around the needle and flush with the fabric.

3 Hold the wrapped thread in place. Gently pull the needle and thread through the fabric. Continue pulling the thread so that the wrapped thread lays flat on the fabric, filling in the space.

4 Finish the bullion knot. Bring the needle back down through the fabric next to the end of the wrapped knot. This creates a single bullion knot.

CAST-ON STITCH

The cast-on stitch is similar to the bullion knot in that it creates a raised knot on the front of the fabric. The cast-on stitch, however, is more rectangular in shape and has a different texture in the stitch.

1 Bring the needle up from the back of the fabric to the front. Choose the length of the cast-on stitch you wish to create and bring the needle back down through the fabric.

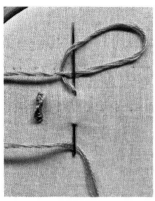

2 **Don't push the needle all the way through the fabric.** Bring it back up next to where the thread is coming out of the fabric. With the needle in the fabric, cross the thread over itself in your fingers, then slide the needle inside the loop. Gently tug the loop so that it casts onto the needle.

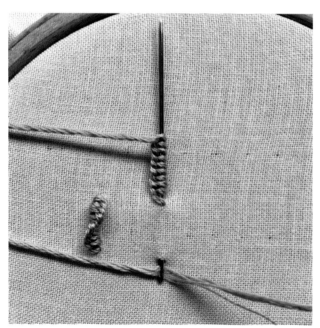

3 **Continue casting stitches on the needle.** Go until the stitches are the length of the space you wish to fill.

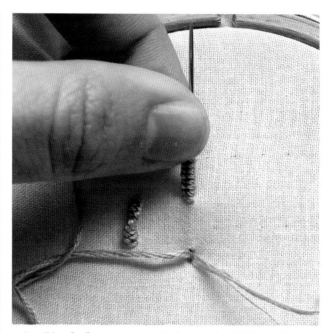

4 **Pinch the cast-on stitches to hold them in place and gently tug the needle and thread.** Pull the threaded needle until the cast-on stitches lay flush with the fabric.

5 **Finish the cast-on stitch.** Bring the needle back down through the fabric where the cast-on stitch started.

CHAIN STITCH

The chain stitch creates a linked chain in a row on the front of the fabric.

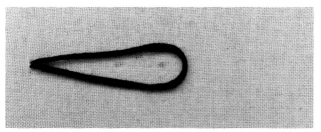

1 **Bring the needle up through the fabric from the back to begin the chain stitch row.** Bring the needle back down through the fabric at the starting point. Gently tug the thread to create an open loop on the front of the fabric in the direction of the chain link.

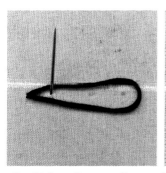
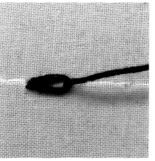

2 **Bring the needle up through the fabric inside the loop at the top point of the chain link.** Gently tug the thread so that the loop is flush with the fabric. This creates the first link in the chain.

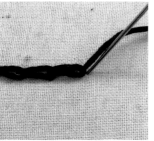

3 **Continue adding links to the desired length.** Bring the needle back down through the fabric inside the previous loop. To finish the chain link row, bring the needle back down through the fabric on the outer edge of the chain link, creating a short, straight stitch to hold the link in place.

CLOSED RAISED HERRINGBONE STITCH

The closed raised herringbone stitch creates a leaf shape that is raised off the fabric for additional depth.

1 **Bring the needle up through the fabric from the back to the front at the base of the leaf.** Then make a short vertical stitch from the bottom of the leaf into the shape. Bring the needle up through the fabric at the top point of the leaf. Slide the needle underneath the short straight stitch.

2 **Gently pull the thread taut to the fabric.** Bring the needle down through the fabric to the right of where the needle came up through the fabric, along the edge of the leaf.

3 **Bring the needle up through the fabric to the
left of the top stitch, along the edge of the
leaf shape.** Moving from the same direction as the
previous stitch, slide the needle underneath the
short straight stitch, so that the thread crosses over
the thread on the front of the fabric.

4 **Gently pull the thread through.** Bring the
needle back down along on the right side of the
stitches, along the outer edge of the leaf. Continue
until the leaf shape is filled.

COLONIAL KNOT

The colonial knot creates a rounded, raised knot on
the front of the fabric. It's similar to the French knot,
but the colonial knot is generally taller.

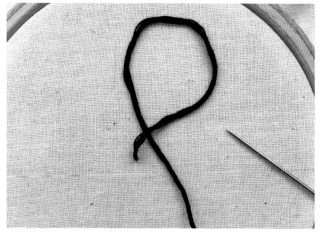

1 **Bring the needle up through the fabric where
you'd like the center of the knot.** Twist the
thread coming out of the fabric so that it creates a
crossed loop.

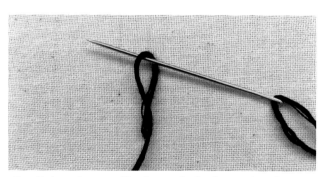

2 **Bring the needle through the loop.** Gently tug
the loop closer to the needle but still loose.

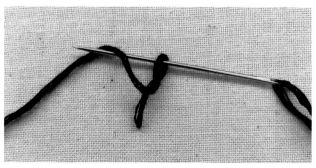

3 **Wrap the thread around the needle.**

4 **Bring the needle back through the fabric.** Before pushing the needle all the way through the fabric, gently tug the wrapped thread so that it is tightly wrapped around the needle and flush with the fabric.

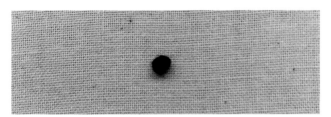

5 **Once it is tight and flush, push the needle all the way through the fabric.** This creates one colonial knot.

COUCHING STITCH

This versatile stitch is good for lines, outlines, or filling. Two threads are needed to stitch the horizontal and vertical parts.

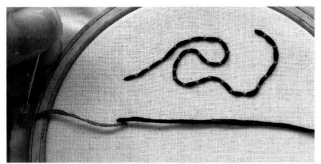

1 **Thread the needle with the thicker of the two threads.** Bring the needle up from the back of the fabric at the start of the line or section. Unthread the needle and lay this thread flat on the fabric in the direction of the line or section to be filled. Rethread and knot the needle with the thinner thread. Bring the thinner thread up from the back of the fabric about ⅛"–¼" (3-6mm) away from the start of the thicker thread.

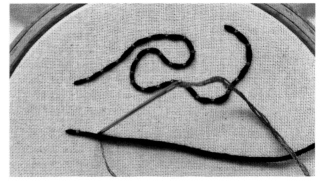

2 **Guide the thicker thread into place.** Then make a short stitch across the thicker thread to tack it into place. Repeat this by working along the thicker thread with spaced out tacking stitches until you're almost at the end of the line or section. Tacking stitches can be spaced out with as many or as few as you'd prefer. I usually make a stitch every ¼" (6mm) along the thicker thread.

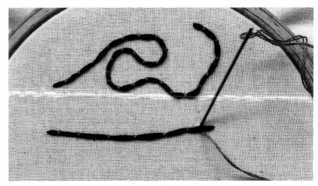

3 **To end the couching stitch, rethread the needle with the thicker thread.** Bring the needle back down through the fabric at the end of the line or section. Knot the thread. Rethread the needle with the thinner thread. Make the last tacking stitch along the thicker thread and knot the thread on the back of the fabric.

DANISH KNOT

The Danish knot creates a raised triangular knot on the front of the fabric.

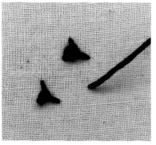 

1 **Bring the needle up through the fabric at the top point of the triangle.** Bring the needle back down through the fabric at the bottom-right corner of the triangle, making a straight stitch.

2 **Bring the needle up through the fabric in the bottom-left corner of the triangle.** Slide the needle under the straight stitch with the tip pointed toward the bottom-left corner.

3 **Gently pull the thread so that it wraps around the straight stitch.** Slide the needle under the straight stitch again, with the tip of the needle pointed toward the bottom-left corner. This time, the tip of the needle should go over the thread coming out of the fabric. Again, gently tug the thread so that it is flush with the fabric.

4 **Create one Danish knot.** Bring the needle back down through the fabric in the bottom-left corner of the triangle.

DETACHED BUTTONHOLE STITCH

The detached buttonhole stitch creates a raised row of stitches on the front of the fabric.

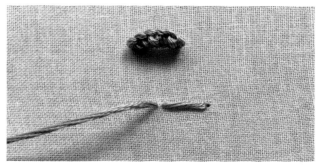

1 **Bring the needle up through the fabric.** Make a straight stitch the length of the detached buttonhole stitch. Bring the needle back up through the fabric at the start of the straight stitch.

 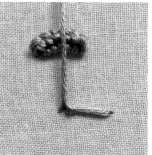

2 **Slide the needle under the straight stitch and over the thread.** Gently tug so that the thread creates a loop around the straight stitch.

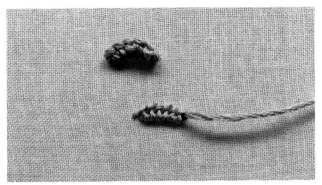

3 **Repeat adding loops to the straight stitch until the entire length is filled.** Once filled, you can either end the stitch or build on top of the looped row that was just created.

4 **This is how to build on top of an existing row.** Slide the needle through the top of the loop closest to where the end of the thread is. Continue making loops in the opposite direction. The more rows added, the more this stitch will extend off the fabric.

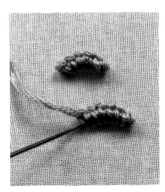

5 **Finish the detached buttonhole stitch.** Come to the end of a row, and bring the needle back down in the hole of the straight stitch.

DETACHED CHAIN STITCH/LAZY DAISY

The detached chain stitch is also known as the lazy daisy. This stitch creates an individual link on the front of the fabric. By creating stitches from the same origin point and continuing in a circle, you can create a daisy.

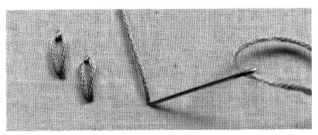

1 **Bring the needle up through the fabric from the back to the front.** Hold the thread in the direction of the detached chain and bring the needle back down through the fabric in the hole of the previous stitch.

2 **Gently tug the thread so that it forms an open loop on the front of the fabric.** Bring the needle up through the fabric, inside the loop, at the top point of the detached chain.

3 **Gently pull the thread so that it forms a link on the front of the fabric.** Bring the needle back through the fabric at the top outer edge of the loop to create a short straight stitch to hold the link in place. This creates one detached chain stitch.

DRIZZLE STITCH

The drizzle stitch creates a packed row of stitches that sticks out from the fabric.

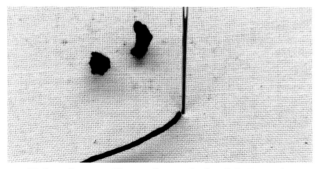

1 **Bring the needle up through the fabric at the base of the drizzle stitch.** Unthread the needle and stitch the needle tip into the fabric next to where the thread is coming out of the fabric.

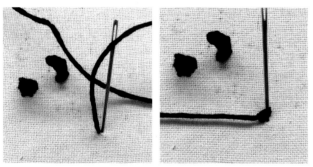

2 **Cast stitches onto the needle.** Do this by creating a crossed loop with the thread and pulling it tightly around the needle.

3 **Cast on the desired number of stitches to the needle.** The more stitches cast on, the taller the drizzle stitch will be.

4 **Thread the needle with the loose end of thread.** With the needle threaded, gently pull the needle through the fabric, creating a single drizzle stitch.

FLY STITCH VARIATIONS

The fly stitch creates a V-shaped stitch. To make the basic fly stitch, I suggest following steps 2–3 of the connected fly stitch.

This book uses two variations of the fly stitch: the closed fly stitch and the connected fly stitch. The closed fly stitch is a great way to fill in a shape with V-shaped stitches next to one another. The connected fly stitch creates a line with Vs spaced along it.

Closed Fly Stitch

1 **Bring the needle up through the fabric at the top point of the closed fly fill section.** Make a straight stitch about one-third of the way down the center of the section that is being filled.

2 **Bring the needle up through the fabric to the left of the top of the straight stitch.** Hold the thread toward the bottom of the straight stitch and bring the needle back down next to the top right of the straight stitch.

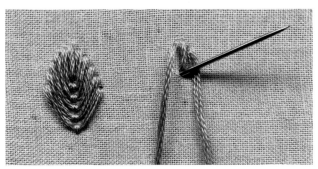

3 **Gently pull the thread so that it creates an open loop on the front of the fabric.** Then bring the needle up at the base of the straight stitch and inside the loop of thread.

4 **Gently tug so that the thread loop becomes flush with the fabric.** Bring the needle back down through the fabric on the outer edge of the *V*, tacking it in place with a short straight stitch.

5 **Continue adding *V*s next to one another until the section is filled.**

Connected Fly Stitch

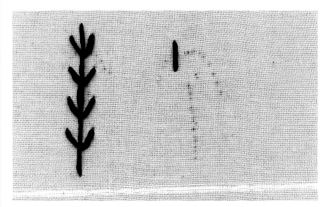

1 **Bring the needle up through the fabric at the top point of the connected fly stitch.** Make a short straight stitch forward along the line of the connected fly stitch.

2 **Bring the needle up through the fabric, slightly away from the left center of the straight stitch.** This will be the top-left point of the *V*. Bring the needle back down through the fabric on the opposite side of the straight stitch. This will be the top-right point of the *V*.

3 **Gently tug the thread so that this creates a loop of thread on the front of the fabric.** Now bring the needle back through the fabric at the bottom of the straight stitch.

4 **Gently tug the thread so that the loop creates a *V* of thread that is flush with the fabric.**

5 **Repeat, adding straight stitches and *V*s until the line of connected fly stitches is complete.** To end the connected fly stitch, make a straight stitch of any desired length.

FRENCH KNOT

The French knot creates a round dot on the front of the fabric. It's similar to the colonial knot, but the French knot is generally fuller. This stitch is all about thread tension, so you might find it helpful to lay your hoop flat on the table, to work with both of your hands.

1 **Bring the needle up through the fabric at the center of the knot.** Pinch the thread in your nondominant hand about 3"–4" (7.5–10cm) from where the thread comes out of the front of the fabric.

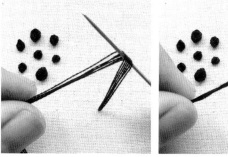 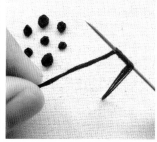

2 **Wrap the thread around the needle.** Keep it in between where the thread is pinched and where it is coming out of the fabric. The more times the thread is wrapped, the larger the knot will be.

3 **Bring the needle back down through the fabric next to where the thread is coming up.**

4 Tighten the thread and finish the knot.

Before pushing the needle all the way through the fabric, gently tug the thread so that it is tightly wrapped around the needle and flush with the fabric. This creates one French knot.

> **Tip**
>
> French knots are all about thread tension. If the thread is loose, the French knot will be loopy. This is also true for the colonial knot and pistil stitch.

GRANITOS STITCH

The granitos stitch creates a raised oval on the front of the fabric.

1 Bring the needle up from the back of the fabric to the front.

Make a short stitch forward, the desired length of the granitos stitch.

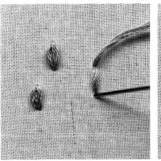

2 Bring the needle back up through the fabric at the start of the straight stitch.

Then go back down through the bottom of the straight stitch. Gently pull the thread close to the fabric, pressing it to the side of the straight stitch.

3 Repeat on the other side, pressing the thread to the left of the stitch.

This creates one granitos stitch.

LONG AND SHORT SATIN STITCH

The long and short satin stitch is great for filling in large areas as well as blending colors together.

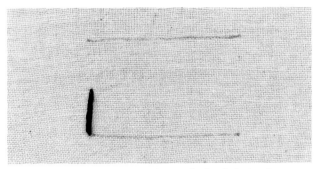

1 Bring the needle up through the fabric.

Start at the bottom of the section that is to be filled. Make a straight stitch into the section.

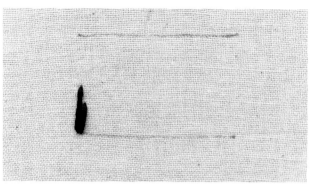

2 **Bring the needle back up next to the start of the first stitch.** Make a stitch that's either shorter or longer than the last stitch.

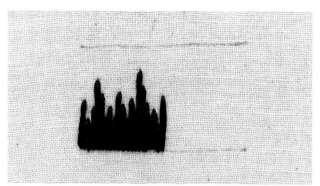

3 **Continue filling in the shape with a horizontal row of stitches that vary in length.**

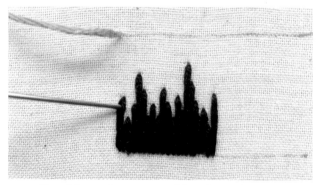

4 **To add another row or blend another color, bring the needle up on the opposite side of the shape.** Then make a straight stitch toward the end of the stitches that are filling the space. To connect the two stitches, bring the needle down into the stitch so that the ends slightly overlap.

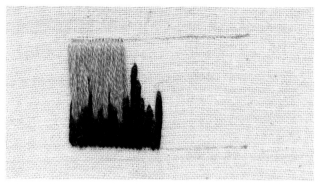

5 **Bring the needle back up through the fabric next to the start of this stitch.** Continue adding stitches in this row, blending the two rows together.

OYSTER STITCH

The oyster stitch combines the twisted chain stitch and the chain stitch to create an intricate oval on the front of the fabric.

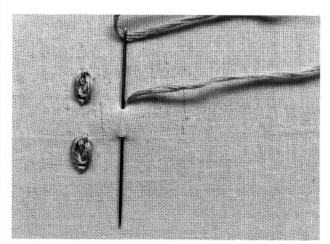

1 **Bring the needle up through the fabric, from the back to the front, at the top point of the oval.** Bring the needle down through the fabric, slightly lower and to the left of where the thread is coming out of the fabric. Before pushing the needle all the way through the fabric, bring the needle back up through the fabric at the bottom length of the oyster stitch, so that the needle is in the fabric.

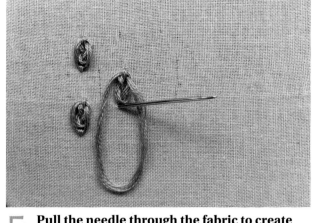

2 **With the needle in the fabric, wrap the thread across the needle.** Then slip under the pointed end of the needle. Gently pull the needle to create the **twisted chain stitch**.

5 **Pull the needle through the fabric to create an open loop on the front of the fabric.** Bring the needle up through the fabric at the base of the twisted chain stitch, inside the loop.

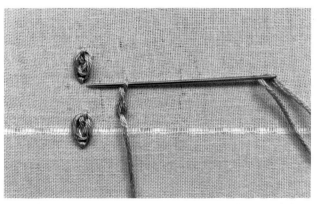

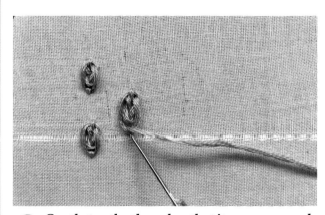

3 **Slide the needle under the top-right tip of the twisted chain stitch.** Gently pull the thread so that it creates a loop to the right of the twisted chain.

6 **Gently tug the thread so that it wraps around the twisted chain stitch and is flush with the fabric.** Finish the chain link by bringing the needle back down through the fabric at the bottom point of the oval on the outer edge of the thread loop. This creates a single oyster stitch.

4 **Bring the needle back down through the fabric inside the loop next to the top right of the twisted chain stitch.** Continue to tug the thread so that the loop on the right is flush with the fabric.

PADDED SATIN STITCH

The padded satin stitch is a satin stitch with padding underneath it. It's slightly more raised and fluffier than the satin stitch.

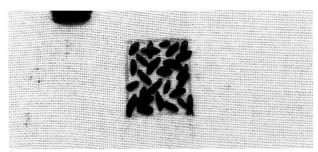

1 **To create the padded satin stitch, fill in the section with a filling stitch.** This can be the seed stitch, back stitch, or the satin stitch filled in using a different direction.

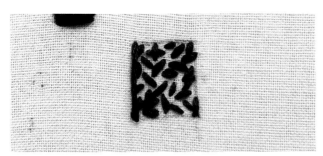

2 **Stitch the satin stitch over the filling stitches.** Bring the needle up from the back of the fabric at the bottom of the section. Create a straight stitch across to the other side of the section.

3 **Continue adding satin stitches.** Bring the needle up next to where the first stitch was started and then go across to the other side. Satin stitches should be close together, almost like they're hugging one another, and fill the section in the same direction.

PISTIL STITCH

The pistil stitch is a French knot with a line attached to it.

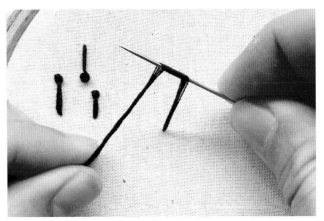

1 **Bring the needle up through the fabric, from the back to the front, at the bottom point of your stitch.** Pinch the thread in your nondominant hand about 3"–4" (7.5–10cm) from where the thread comes out of the front of the fabric. In between where the thread is pinched and where it is coming out of the fabric, wrap the thread around the needle. The more times the thread is wrapped, the larger the knot will be.

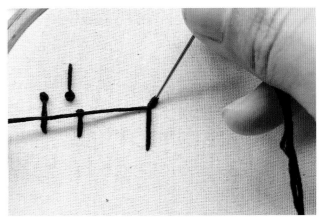

2 **After the thread is wrapped, bring the needle back down through the fabric at the top point of the pistil stitch.** Before pushing the needle all the way through the fabric, gently tug the thread so that it is tightly wrapped around the needle and flush with the fabric. This creates a single pistil stitch.

RADIAL SATIN STITCH

The radial satin stitch creates a smooth fill that is stitched around a central point.

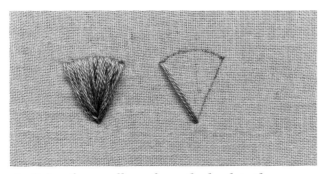

1 **Bring the needle up from the back to the front along the outer edge of the radial shape.** Make a straight satin stitch down toward the point of radiation.

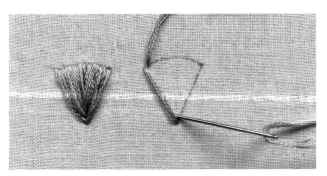

2 **Bring the needle back up along the outer edge of the shape, next to the previous stitch.** Again, stitch toward the point of radiation, however, this stitch should be slightly shorter than the last one. Tuck the end of the stitch underneath the thread of the previous stitch.

3 **Repeat, making a shorter stitch next to the last.**

4 **Make a longer stitch next to these three stitches that goes from the outer edge to the point of radiation.** Then repeat the shorter and longer stitches as you stitch around the shape, until it is filled.

REVERSE CHAIN STITCH

The reverse chain stitch is similar to the chain stitch, creating a raised chain link on the front of the fabric. These stitches are interchangeable. While I prefer the reverse chain to the chain stitch, this version requires more space to create, so sometimes using one or the other is a better fit for the pattern and space that is being filled.

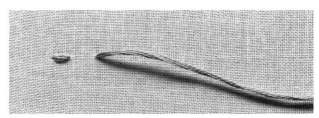

1 **The reverse chain stitch row is started with one short back stitch.** Similar to the back stitch, leave a space away from the previous stitch, then bring the needle up through the fabric.

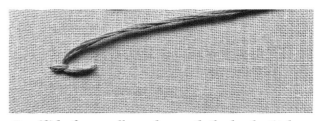

2 **Slide the needle underneath the back stitch.** Gently tug the thread so that it is flush with the fabric. Then bring the needle back down in the hole of the stitch, closing the chain link.

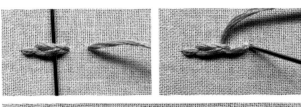

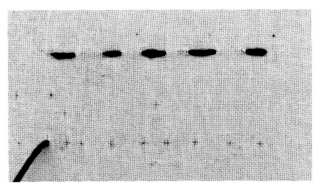

3 **Continue to add links to the chain by bringing the needle up a stitch's length away from the previous link.** Slide the needle under both strands of the link. Then close the loop by bringing the needle back down through the hole of the stitch.

> **Tip**
>
> If the needle tip is getting caught in the stitches, flip the needle around and slide the eye under the thread. The eye is blunter and will help the needle from getting caught in the thread and splitting it apart.

RUNNING STITCH

The running stitch creates a dashed line. I like to use this for attaching fabrics together and for gathering the fabric on the back of an embroidery.

1 **Bring the needle up through the fabric, from the back to the front, where the dashed line will start.**

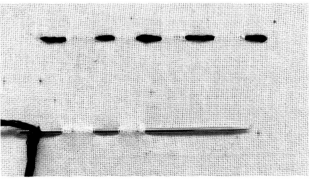

2 **Weave the needle in and out of the fabric.** Then gently tug the needle and thread through the fabric to create the dashed line.

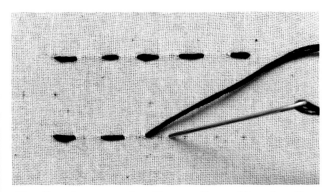

3 **Continue weaving the needle and tugging the thread until the dashed line is the desired length.** To finish the running stitch, bring the needle back down through the fabric, about a stitch's length away, making the last running stitch in the row.

> **Tip**
>
> Sometimes weaving the needle in and out of the fabric is challenging. Create one stitch at a time by making a short stitch forward, leaving a space away from that stitch, then making another stitch forward along the row.

SATIN STITCH

The satin stitch creates a solid fill of smooth color with all the stitches being made in the same direction.

1 **Bring the needle up from the back of the fabric to the front at the bottom of the section.** Create a straight stitch across to the other side of the section.

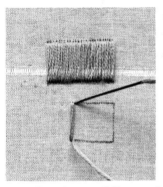
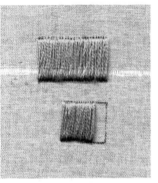

2 **Continue adding satin stitches by bringing the needle up next to where the first stitch was started.** Satin stitches should be close together, almost like they're hugging one another, and fill the section in the same direction. It's okay if they overlap.

SEED STITCH

The seed stitch creates short stitches in different directions. It looks like a scattering of seeds or confetti.

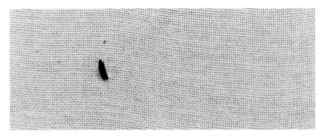

1 **Bring the needle up from the back of the fabric to the front.** Make a short stitch forward in any direction to fill the space.

2 **Leave a space and bring the needle back up through the fabric.** Make another short stitch forward in a different direction.

3 **Continue filling the space with short, small stitches that go in different directions.**

Tip To add more texture, densely fill the section by overlapping the seed stitches.

SPLIT BACK STITCH

The split back stitch creates a line of stitches that connect into themselves.

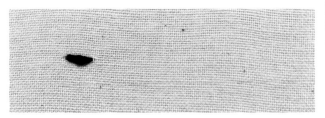

1 Create one short back stitch along the row. Bring the needle up from the back of the fabric to the front a stitch's length away from the starting point of the line and back down at the beginning of the line.

2 Leave a space away from the previous stitch, along the line and bring the needle back up through the fabric. Bring the needle back down through the fabric in the middle of the last stitch, splitting the thread of the stitch.

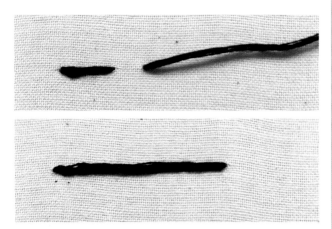

3 Continue leaving a space and filling it in. Bring the needle down in the middle of the last stitch until the line is complete.

STEM STITCH

The stem stitch creates a coiled rope on the front of the fabric.

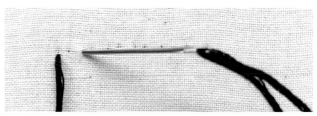

1 Bring the needle up from the back of the fabric to the front at the start of the line. Hold the thread off to one side of the line and bring the needle back down through the fabric a stitch's length away (about ⅛"–¼" [3–6mm]).

2 Keep the loop of thread on the front of the fabric. Bring the needle back up through the fabric in between where the thread is coming in and out of the fabric, along the same line. Then gently tug the thread loop so that it is flush with the fabric.

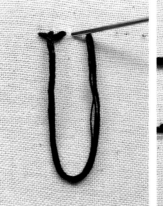 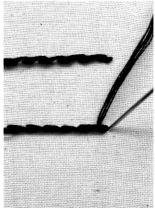

3 Continue along the line. Hold the thread off to the same side, bring the needle back down through the fabric a stitch's length away, then back up through the fabric in between where the thread is coming in and out of the fabric. To finish the stem line, bring the needle down through the fabric in the hole of the last stitch.

STRAIGHT STITCH

The straight stitch is a single straight line. It is sometimes referred to as a single satin stitch.

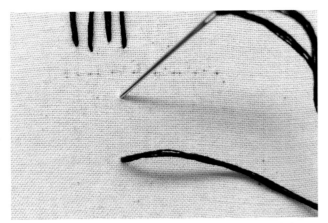

1 **Bring the needle up from the back of the fabric at the bottom point of the straight stitch.**

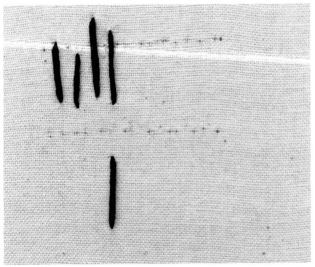

2 **Bring the needle back down through the fabric at the top point of the straight stitch.** This creates a single straight stitch.

TULIP STITCH

The tulip stitch creates a tulip-shaped flower on the front of the fabric.

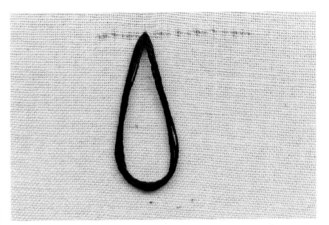

1 **Bring the needle up through the fabric, from the back to the front, at the top point of the tulip stitch.** Then bring the needle back down in the hole of that stitch, creating an open loop on the front of the fabric.

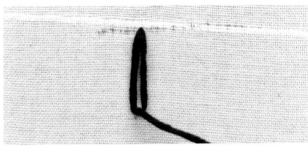

2 **Bring the needle up through the fabric inside the loop, at the base of the tulip.** Gently tug the thread so that the loop is flush with the fabric.

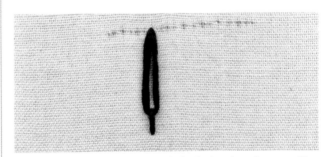

3 **Create a straight stitch by bringing the needle down on the outside of the loop to hold it in place.** This is similar to the detached chain (or lazy daisy) stitch; however, the straight stitch is longer.

4 **Add the *V* shapes to the tulip stitch.** Bring the needle up through the fabric to the right of the link. Then slide the needle underneath the straight stitch of the link and bring the needle back down through the fabric on the other side of the link, parallel to where the opposite stitch started.

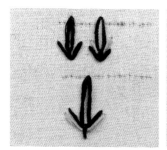
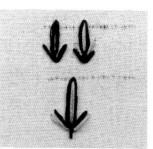

Tip Add additional color and intricacy to the tulip stitch! Use another color to add an additional *V* shape to the base of the tulip and fill the link in with a straight stitch.

TURKEY WORK STITCH

The turkey work stitch creates a fringe on the front of the fabric. For this stitch, you do not want to add a knot to the end of the thread.

1 **Bring the needle from the front of the fabric to the back at the base of the first row of fringe.** Pull the thread so that a short tail is formed on the front of the fabric. Then bring the needle up through the fabric to the left of the base of the tail.

2 **Create a short stitch forward to lock the tail in place.**

3 **Bring the needle up through the fabric in the same place the tail is coming out of the fabric.** Hold a loop of thread on the front of the fabric and bring the needle down through the fabric a short distance away from the last stitch.

4 **Bring the needle up in the hole of the last stitch.** Create a short stitch forward that covers the bottom of the loop to lock it in place.

5 **Continue adding loops of fringe to the horizontal row.** When the section is filled with turkey work rows, trim the loops to create the desired length of fringe.

WEAVE STITCH/WOVEN STITCH

The woven or weave stitch creates a grid pattern on the front of the fabric.

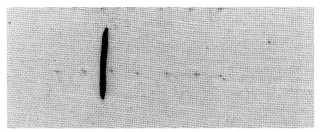

1 **Bring the needle up from the back of the fabric at the bottom corner of the section that will be filled.** Make a straight stitch across to the opposite side and gently tug the thread flush with the fabric.

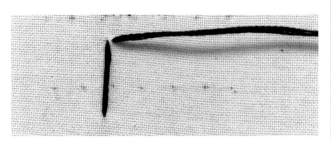

2 **Leave a small space on the same side where the needle went down through the fabric.** Bring the needle back up through the fabric. Then make a short stitch across to the other side of the shape.

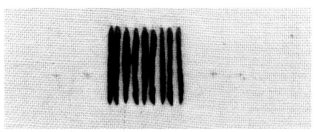

3 **Continue filling in the shape with straight parallel lines that are close to one another.**

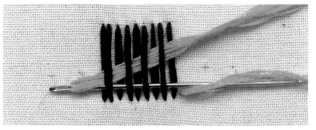

4 **Weave in the perpendicular rows.** Bring the threaded needle up through the fabric near the bottom corner of the section. Flip the needle around and weave the eye of the needle over, under, over, under the lines of thread, working the needle across to the opposite side.

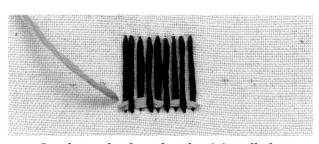

5 **Gently tug the thread so that it is pulled through the rows and is flush with the fabric.** Then bring the needle down through the fabric to end the row. Bring the needle back up through the fabric slightly above the row that just ended.

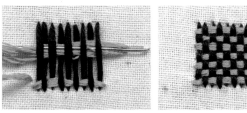

6 **Weave the needle through the thread in an alternating pattern from the previous row.** Continue adding woven rows until the section is filled.

Tip

If the vertical and horizontal rows are spaced out, there will be spaces in the grid. For a tighter grid, stitch the rows closer together.

WHEATEAR STITCH

The wheatear stitch is a variation of the chain stitch. It looks like a connected row with stalks of wheat.

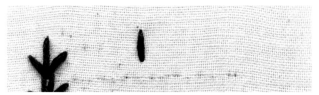

1 **Bring the needle up at the top point of the row of stitches.** Create a short straight stitch down the line.

2 **Add the prongs on either side of the straight stitch.** Bring the needle up to the right and slightly away from the center of the straight stitch. Then make a diagonal stitch by bring the needle back down through the bottom of the straight stitch. Repeat on the left.

3 **Make the looped part of the wheatear stitch.** Bring the needle up a stitch's length away from the bottom of where the three stitches connect. Then slide the needle underneath all three stitches and gently tug the thread so that it lays flat on the fabric.

4 **Bring the needle back down through the hole of the stitch you just made, to close the loop.**

5 **Continue adding to the row of wheatear stitches by creating the diagonal stitches on either side of the loop.** Then leave a space along the row and fill it in with the loop by sliding the needle underneath the diagonal stitches and previous loop. Continue along the row until you've created the desired length.

WHIPPED BACK STITCH

The whipped back stitch creates a line similar to a candy cane on the front of the fabric.

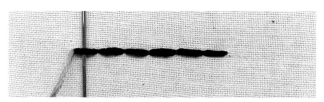

1 **Create a line with the back stitch.** Bring the needle up through the fabric, from the back, in the hole of the first back stitch. Slide the needle underneath the first back stitch. Be sure to only slide under the thread and not stitch through the fabric.

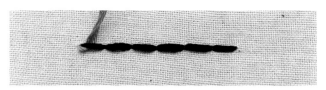

2 **Gently pull the thread so that it is flush with the fabric.**

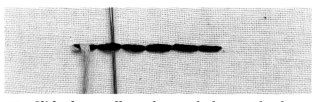

3 **Slide the needle underneath the next back stitch in the row.** Be sure to slide the needle in the same direction so that the whipped thread wraps around the back stitches.

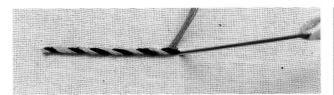

4 **Work down the line of back stiches until the end.** At the end of the line, bring the needle back down through the fabric in the hole of the last back stitch.

WOVEN PICOT STITCH

The woven picot stitch creates a three-dimensional triangle on the front of the fabric. The triangle is attached at the base and pops away from the fabric. This stitch uses a lot of thread. It is important to have a long length of thread when creating the woven picot because you cannot add thread as you go.

1 **Place a long pin into the fabric at the top point of the triangle.** Bring it up through the fabric at the bottom center of the triangle. Bring the needle up through the fabric from the back in a bottom corner of the triangle.

2 **Wrap the thread around the top of the pin.** Bring the needle back down through the fabric in the other bottom corner of the triangle. Gently tug the thread so that it is flush with the fabric. This will outline the triangle with thread.

3 **Bring the needle up through the fabric next to the pin, in the bottom center of the triangle.** Wrap the thread around the top of the pin. This will look like a line coming up the center of the triangle. The stitch outline is complete.

4 **Flip the needle around and work with the eye of the needle.** Glide the needle over, under, and over the three strands of the triangle; move in the opposite direction of the thread from where it emerges at the top of the pin. In the photo, the thread is on the right, so I wove the thread through the strands to the left.

6 **Weave back through the strands in the opposite direction, going under, over, under the three strands of thread.** Continue weaving until the triangle is entirely filled and the rows are tightly packed against each other.

5 **After weaving the needle through, gently tug so that the thread is close to the top of the triangle.** The first few rows of weaving should be very tight to fill in the top portion of the triangle. All rows after that will be looser to keep the triangular shape.

7 **End the woven picot stitch by finishing a woven row.** Bring the needle back down through the fabric at the base of the triangle. Knot the thread on the back and then remove the pin to see the woven picot stitch pop away from the fabric!

Tip After the outline is created, the only time the needle will go back down through the fabric is when the stitch is finished. Do not bring the needle down through the fabric when weaving the rows, otherwise the stitch won't pop off the fabric.

Projects

Are you ready to stitch a landscape? These projects include 20 different landscapes inspired by my travels and favorite places. You'll explore deserts, mountains, the tropics, and more. The projects are arranged from beginner to advanced. As you work your way through these designs, you will get to explore different stitches and create beautiful and textural landscapes.

Joshua Tree

SKILL LEVEL: BEGINNER

Joshua Tree National Park has long been on my bucket list of places to visit. During the spring of 2020, my husband and I made plans to go, but as you can probably guess, that didn't happen. Instead, I drooled over photos and designed this landscape to stitch.

Here's what you'll need to create this design:

- Pattern (page 148)
- 5" (12.7cm) wood embroidery hoop
- Cotton fabric (I used: Speckled in Parchment by

- Ruby Star Society = tan; Jetty Collection #19068-107 by Carolyn Friedlander = pink)
- #5 embroidery needle

- DMC colors: 301, 422, 435, 898, 3345, 3347, 3776, 3830, and 3858
- Scissors
- Pencil or erasable pen
- Transfer paper (optional)

ILLUSTRATED STITCH GUIDE

This diagram shows what colors and stitches will be used within this design. Follow the instructions for the layer order, details, and tips on each section.

For detailed instructions on how to create each stitch, see the Stitch Glossary starting on page 20.

DMC 3345 & 3347 + Straight Stitch

DMC 435 + Reverse Chain Stitch

DMC 422 + Long and Short Satin Stitch

DMC 3776 + Satin Stitch

DMC 898 + Long and Short Satin Stitch

DMC 301 + Back Stitch

DMC 3830 & 3858 + Straight Stitch

Using different fabric makes the desert design unique. The left evokes a sunset while the right feels like a hot summer day.

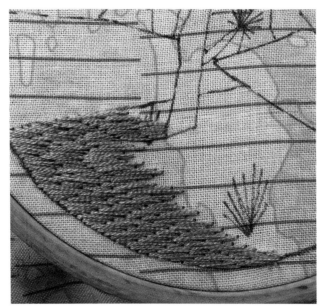

1 **Bottom landscape.** 3 strands of DMC 422 + Long and Short Satin Stitch. Use horizontal stitches to create a flat and somewhat rough texture.

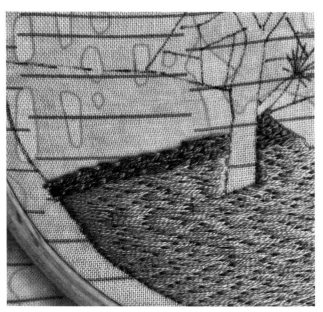

2 **Left landscape.** 3 strands of DMC 435 + Reverse Chain Stitch. Use the last landscape layer as a guide for what angle to stitch your first row of stitches. Be sure to skip the tree trunk when filling in this layer.

3 **Middle-right landscape.** 3 strands of DMC 301 + Back Stitch. Use the first layer as a guide for the angle of your first row of stitches. Offset each row of stitches (like rows of bricks) to create texture within the layer without drawing attention to the points where the stitches meet.

4 **Tree trunk.** 4 strands of DMC 898 + Long and Short Satin Stitch. Stitch each trunk section from bottom to top, following the angle of that section. Using this stitch on the tree trunk adds a rough bark effect, while the vertical stitches differentiate it from the other layers.

5 **Top landscape.** 3 strands of DMC 3776 + Satin Stitch. Each section in this rock face should be stitched in a different direction from those around it to make the layer look as if rocks are piled on top of one another.

6 **Leaves.** 2 strands of DMC 3345 + Straight Stitch for the first layer of leaves. Stitch every other leaf to alternate the color of the leaves. Start at the outer edge of the leaf and bring the needle down toward the center point to create the fanned effect. 2 strands of DMC 3347 + Straight Stitch for the second layer of leaves on each branch.

7 **Shrubs.** 3 strands of DMC 3858 + Straight Stitch for first layer of shrubs. Start at the outer edges and bring the needle down toward the center of the plant. 3 strands of DMC 3830 + Straight Stitch for the second layer of shrubs. Using a second, similar color within leaves also adds to the depth of design.

8 **To finish your design in the hoop, see page 146.**

Where the Forest Meets the Beach

The Oregon coast was the inspiration for this project!
Almost every year, my husband, our pups, and I take a trip to
Cannon Beach to enjoy the forested drive and sandy beaches.

Here's what you'll need to create this design:

- Pattern (page 148)
- 6" x 4" (15.2 x 10.2cm) oval wood embroidery hoop
- Cotton fabric (I used Dash Flow in Allure by Dear Stella)

- #5 embroidery needle
- DMC colors: 8, 453, 543, 613, 645, 926, 935, 937, 3051, 3363, 3364, 3752, and 3782
- Scissors

- Pencil or erasable pen
- Transfer paper (optional)

ILLUSTRATED STITCH GUIDE

This diagram shows what colors and stitches will be used within this design. Follow the instructions for the layer order, details, and tips on each section.

For detailed instructions on how to create each stitch, see the Stitch Glossary starting on page 20.

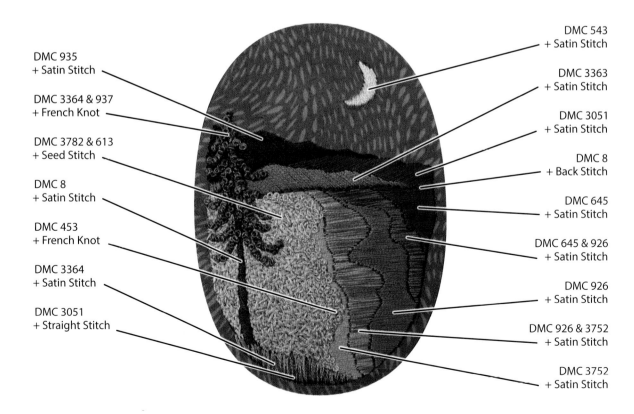

DMC 935
+ Satin Stitch

DMC 3364 & 937
+ French Knot

DMC 3782 & 613
+ Seed Stitch

DMC 8
+ Satin Stitch

DMC 453
+ French Knot

DMC 3364
+ Satin Stitch

DMC 3051
+ Straight Stitch

DMC 543
+ Satin Stitch

DMC 3363
+ Satin Stitch

DMC 3051
+ Satin Stitch

DMC 8
+ Back Stitch

DMC 645
+ Satin Stitch

DMC 645 & 926
+ Satin Stitch

DMC 926
+ Satin Stitch

DMC 926 & 3752
+ Satin Stitch

DMC 3752
+ Satin Stitch

The texture of the seafoam contrasts nicely with the smooth stitches used for the ocean.

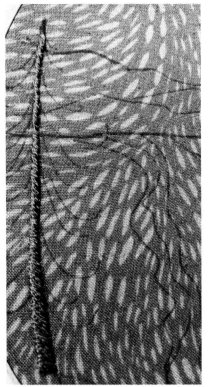

2 **Top mountains.** 3 strands of DMC 935 + Satin Stitch for left mountain. Stitch this section at a diagonal, following the slope of the mountainside. Be sure to stitch around the tree branches. 3 strands of DMC 3051 + Satin Stitch for right mountain. Follow the angle of the mountainside when filling in this section.

1 **Tree trunk.** 3 strands of DMC 8 + Satin Stitch. Fill the trunk with stitches at a 45-degree diagonal.

3 **Bottom mountain.** 3 strands of DMC 3363 + Satin Stitch. Stitch in the same direction as the top-left mountainside and around the tree branches. 3 strands of DMC 8 + Back Stitch for the thin line along the bottom of the mountainside. Stitch until it connects to the tree branches.

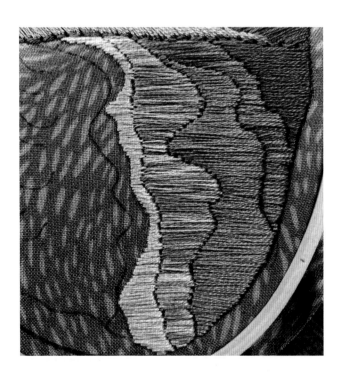

4 **Right water.** 3 strands of DMC 645 + Satin Stitch. These stitches should be created horizontally.

5 **Middle-right water.** 1 strand of DMC 645 & 2 strands of DMC 926 + Satin Stitch. Continue stitching this section with horizontal stitches.

6 **Middle water.** 3 strands of DMC 926 + Satin Stitch. Continue stitching this section with horizontal stitches.

7 **Middle-left water.** 2 strands of DMC 926 & 1 strand of DMC 3752 + Satin Stitch. Continue filling this section with horizontal stitches.

8 **Left water.** 3 strands of DMC 3752 + Satin Stitch. Continue filling this section with horizontal stitches.

10 **Sand.** 2 strands of DMC 3782 and 1 strand of DMC 613 + Seed Stitch. Fill in around the tree and leaves.

11 **Grass.** 3 strands of DMC 3364 + Satin Stitch for the base layer of grass. Make stitches vertical, with the tops slightly overlapping the other sections in varying lengths. 2 strands of DMC 3051 + Straight Stitch for the darker strands of grass on top. Using another color will add depth to the grassy section.

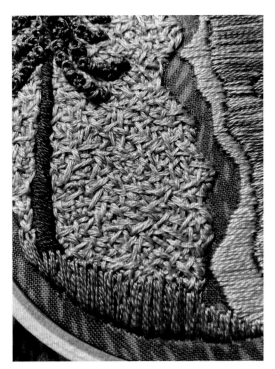

9 **Leaves.** 2 strands of DMC 937 & 1 strand of DMC 3364 + French Knot. Fill in the branches of the tree.

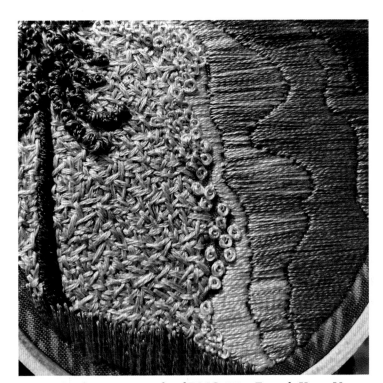

13 **Moon.** 3 strands of DMC 543 + Satin Stitch. To keep the curved crescent of the moon, create the satin stitches at the 135-degree angle.

14 **To finish your design in the hoop, see page 146.**

12 **Seafoam.** 2 strands of DMC 453 + French Knot. Vary the number of times the thread is wrapped around the needle when making the French knots to create more texture and dimension along the waterfront.

Mojave Hues

SKILL LEVEL: BEGINNER

I grew up in the desert of Washington state, so I've always had a love for the Mojave Desert in California. This project was inspired by those earthy desert colors and many layers of rock that come to mind from my childhood.

Here's what you'll need to create this design:

- Pattern (page 149)
- 6" (15.2cm) wood embroidery hoop
- Cotton fabric (I used: Haze Rust by Cotton + Steel = rust; Unruly Nature by Ruby Star Society = yellow)
- #5 embroidery needle
- Long sewing pins
- DMC colors: 28, 301, 310, C436, 733, 746, 918, 920, 921, 3750, 3752, 3776, 3857, and 3858
- Scissors
- Pencil or erasable pen
- Transfer paper (optional)

ILLUSTRATED STITCH GUIDE

This diagram shows what colors and stitches will be used within this design. Follow the instructions for the layer order, details, and tips on each section.

For detailed instructions on how to create each stitch, see the Stitch Glossary starting on page 20.

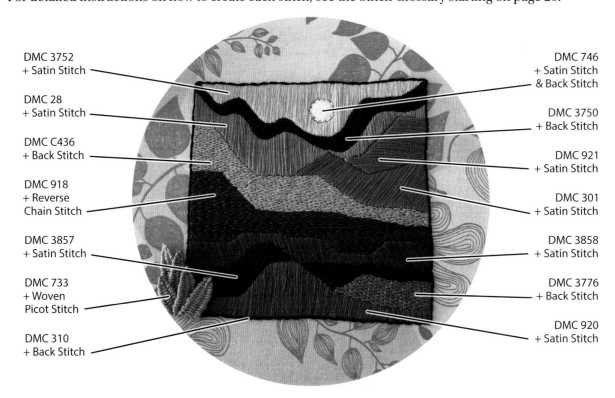

DMC 3752 + Satin Stitch

DMC 28 + Satin Stitch

DMC C436 + Back Stitch

DMC 918 + Reverse Chain Stitch

DMC 3857 + Satin Stitch

DMC 733 + Woven Picot Stitch

DMC 310 + Back Stitch

DMC 746 + Satin Stitch & Back Stitch

DMC 3750 + Back Stitch

DMC 921 + Satin Stitch

DMC 301 + Satin Stitch

DMC 3858 + Satin Stitch

DMC 3776 + Back Stitch

DMC 920 + Satin Stitch

The floral print on the left design frames the embroidery nicely. On the right, the orange print is reminiscent of patterns often used in the Southwest.

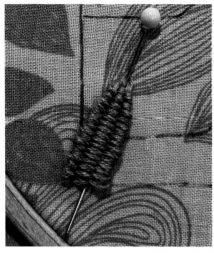 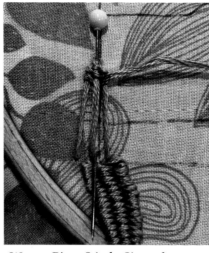 

1 **3D leaves.** 6 strands of DMC 733 + Woven Picot Stitch. Since they overlap, start with the plant leaves closest to the front and work your way backward. Pinning the finished leaves out of the way as the others are stitched will help keep them from getting caught in the needle and thread.

2 **Bottom landscape.** 3 strands of DMC 920 + Satin Stitch. Stitch this section with vertical stitches.

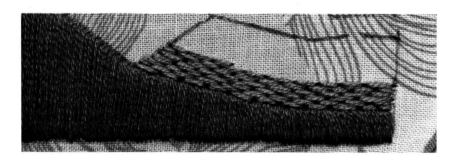

3 **Bottom-right landscape.** 3 strands of DMC 3776 + Back Stitch. Start at the bottom of the layer and create rows like a brick wall as the shape is filled. Offsetting the stitches will disguise where the stitches connect in each row.

4 **Bottom-left landscape.** 3 strands of DMC 3857 + Satin Stitch. This layer is split by the bottom landscape layer into two sections. The stitches should be stitched on the diagonal to help differentiate them from the other layers.

5 **Middle landscape.** 3 strands of DMC 3858 + Satin Stitch. This layer should be stitched at a diagonal opposite from the layer below it to add definition between the layers.

6 **Top landscape.** 4 strands of DMC 918 + Reverse Chain Stitch. Start at the bottom of this section, filling with horizontal rows across the layer.

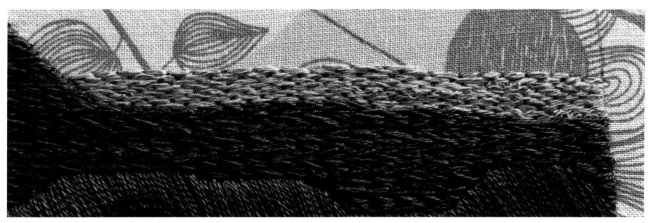

7 **Left mountain.** 3 strands of DMC C436 + Back Stitch. Start at the bottom of this section, filling with horizontal rows across. Offset each row like a brick wall.

> *Tip*
> Etoile thread is a little stretchier than the standard cotton thread due to the metallic sparkle in it. Because it has some stretch, I find it helpful to cut a shorter length of thread and tug gently so that my thread doesn't stretch or break.

8 Right mountains. 3 strands of DMC 301 + Satin Stitch for the middle mountain. Fill this section with diagonal stitches. 3 strands of DMC 921 + Satin Stitch for the top mountain. This layer will be stitched horizontally to distinguish it from the previous layer.

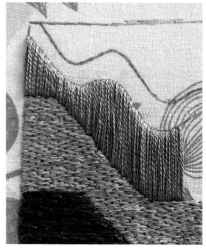

9 Bottom sky. 3 strands of DMC 28 + Satin Stitch. Use vertical stitches.

10 Moon. 3 strands of DMC 746 + Satin Stitch to fill the circle. Circles are surprisingly hard to keep circular so don't stress if yours isn't as circular as you'd hoped. 3 strands of DMC 746 + Back Stitch to outline the circle. Outlines cover up imperfections and can even out a shape.

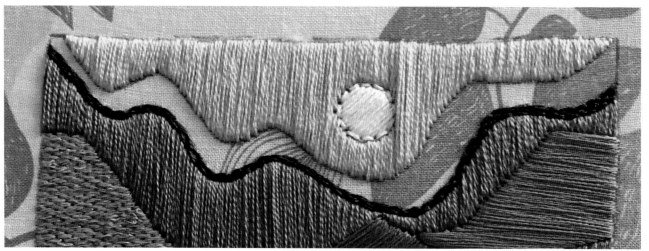

11 Top sky. 3 strands of DMC 3752 + Satin Stitch. This section will also be stitched vertically.

12 Middle sky. 3 strands of DMC 3750 + Back Stitch. Stitches should be made horizontally, following the shape. Offset each row like a brick wall so that it's not obvious where the stitches connect in each row.

13 **Landscape square outline.** 3 strands of DMC 310 + Back Stitch. Start at the plant and stitch around the square.

14 **To finish your design in the hoop, see page 146.**

Hidden Beach Cove

SKILL LEVEL: BEGINNER

A trip to Tulum, Mexico, inspired this tropical pattern.
While visiting the Tulum Archaeological Zone, I was inspired by a little path
between the surrounding rock face that led down to the beach.

Here's what you'll need to create this design:

- Pattern (page 149)
- 4" (10.2cm) wood embroidery hoop
- Cotton fabric (I used First Light in Sono Peach Cream by Ruby Star Society)

- #5 embroidery needle
- DMC colors: 7, 319, 581, 712, 904, 927, 935, 937, 3031, 3371, and 3782
- Scissors

- Pencil or erasable pen
- Transfer paper (optional)

ILLUSTRATED STITCH GUIDE

This diagram shows what colors and stitches will be used within this design. Follow the instructions for the layer order, details, and tips on each section.

For detailed instructions on how to create each stitch, see the Stitch Glossary starting on page 20.

DMC 927 + Long and Short Satin Stitch

DMC 712 + French Knot

DMC 581 + French Knot

DMC 937 + French Knot

DMC 3782 + Satin Stitch

DMC 904 + French Knot

DMC 935 + Connected Fly Stitch

DMC 3371 + Stem Stitch

DMC 3031 + Satin Stitch

DMC 7 + Satin Stitch

DMC 319 + Straight Stitch

DMC 3782 + Long and Short Satin Stitch

A sandy print further evokes the feeling of the beach.

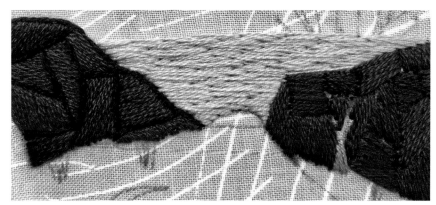

1 **Palm tree trunks.** 3 strands of DMC 7 + Satin Stitch. Stitch these sections at a downward angle.

2 **Water.** 3 strands of DMC 927 + Long and Short Satin Stitch. Fill in this section with horizontal stitches. Using this stitch creates ripples in the water and makes it easier to add overlapping stitches.

3 **Rocks.** 3 strands of DMC 3031 + Satin Stitch to fill in rocks. Each section should be stitched in a different direction. This helps define each rock face and add definition. 2 strands of DMC 3371 + Stem Stitch to fill in the lines between the rock sections. This will help cover any gaps in between stitched rock face sections as well as define each section.

4 **Palm tree leaves.** 3 strands of DMC 935 + Connected Fly Stitch. Start at the top of the palm leaf and work toward the stem. Because some of the leaves overlap, stitch the leaves furthest back first, then stitch on top of them for the leaves that are closer. Continue with the stem stitch to attach the palm leaves to the tree trunks.

5 **Sand dunes.** 3 strands of DMC 3782 + Satin Stitch. Stitch these at an angle to make it easier fill in the wiggly sections.

6 **Right sand.** 3 strands of DMC 3782 + Long and Short Satin Stitch. Use the angle of where the sand meets the rock face as a guide for the slant of the stitches in this section. Stitching at this angle will help with perspective and make the design look less flat.

7 **Middle greenery.** 3 strands of DMC 904 + French Knot. Overlap French knots for a solid fill, additional depth, and texture. Wrapping thread around the needle in differing amounts will also create larger (more thread wraps) and smaller knots (less thread wraps).

8 **Three greenery sections.** 3 strands of DMC 937 + French Knot.

9 **Remaining greenery.** 3 strands of DMC 581 + French Knot.

10 **Seafoam.** 2 strands of DMC 712 + French Knot. Fill in the small space between the greenery and the water.

11 **Shells.** 2 strands of DMC 712 + French Knot. Add dots along the sand on the right. Add as many or as few as you'd like!

12 **Grass.** 3 strands of DMC 319 + Straight Stitch. Add grass to the sandy area to the right and along the bottom of the rock face to the left. Vary the length of the stitches to create depth and variation with the grass. Add as many or as few as you'd like!

13 **To finish your design in the hoop, see page 146.**

Mountains at Sunset

SKILL LEVEL: BEGINNER

From a few blocks over from my house, you can see Mount Rainier.
This project was inspired by the colorful sunsets I often see
while out on evening walks with my pups.

Here's what you'll need to create this design:

- Pattern (page 150)
- 5" (12.7cm) wood embroidery hoop
- Cotton fabric (I used Natural from Kona® Cotton)
- #5 embroidery needle
- DMC colors: Blanc, 24, 28, 168, 169, 316, 500, 734, 745, 754, 898, and 3740
- Scissors
- Pencil or crasable pen
- Transfer paper (optional)

ILLUSTRATED STITCH GUIDE

This diagram shows what colors and stitches will be used within this design. Follow the instructions for the layer order, details, and tips on each section.

For detailed instructions on how to create each stitch, see the Stitch Glossary starting on page 20.

DMC 745
+ Satin Stitch

DMC 316
+ Satin Stitch

DMC 28
+ Back Stitch

DMC 3740
+ Back Stitch

DMC 168
+ Long and Short
Satin Stitch

DMC 734
+ Seed Stitch

DMC 754
+ Satin Stitch

DMC 24
+ Satin Stitch

DMC 168
+ Long and Short
Satin Stitch

DMC Blanc
+ Long and Short
Satin Stitch

DMC 169
+ Long and Short
Satin Stitch

DMC 500
+ Straight Stitch

DMC 898
+ Stem Stitch

Because this embroidery design covers most of the hoop, I choose a fabric that wouldn't distract.

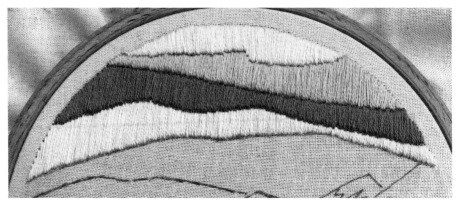

1 Top sunset. 3 strands of DMC 745 + Satin Stitch. Stitches should be vertical and very close together, almost like they're hugging on another. It is fine to overlap. You just want a flat, solid fill of color.

2 Top-middle sunset. 3 strands of DMC 754 + Satin Stitch. This layer will be stitched vertically.

3 Bottom-middle sunset. 3 strands of DMC 316 + Satin Stitch. This layer will be stitched vertically.

4 Bottom sunset. 3 strands of DMC 24 + Satin Stitch. This layer will be stitched vertically.

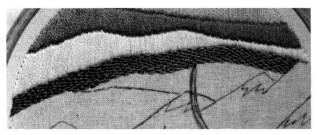

5 Top distant mountain. 3 strands of DMC 28 + Back Stitch. The rows should be stitched horizontally. By offsetting each row of back stitches like bricks, the rows will blend together.

6 Bottom distant mountain. 3 strands of DMC 3740 + Back Stitch. This layer will be stitched horizontally.

7 Snowcaps on the top mountains. 3 strands of DMC Blanc + Long and Short Satin Stitch. These stitches should be made at an angle, following the slant of the mountain range.

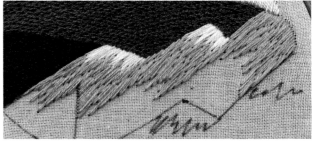

8 Top mountains. 3 strands of DMC 168 + Long and Short Satin Stitch. Just like the snowcaps, use the slant of the mountain as a guide to fill in the shape at an angle. The directional stitches will help keep the steep feel of the mountain and make it easier to blend rows of stitches together. Don't forget to stitch around the trees that overlap the mountains! This will make it easier to stitch them later.

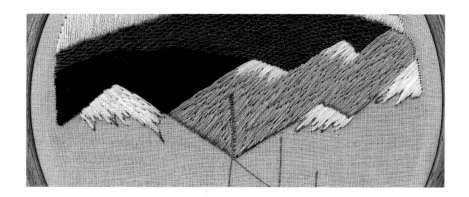

9 **Snowcaps on right and left mountains.** 3 strands of DMC Blanc + Long and Short Satin Stitch.

10 **Right mountains.** 3 strands of DMC 169 + Long and Short Satin Stitch.

11 **Left mountain.** 3 strands of DMC 168 + Long and Short Satin Stitch.

12 **Tree trunks.** 6 strands of DMC 898 + Stem Stitch. Depending on how much space is left when stitching, this could be a single line or a few lines next to one another.

13 **Branches.** 3 strands of DMC 500 + Straight Stitch. Stitch at an angle. You can add as many or as few branches as you'd like. To add depth to the trees, have some straight stitches overlap the trunk, others end in the middle of the trunk, and some end behind the trunk.

14 **Meadow.** 3 strands of DMC 734 + Seed Stitch. To create a robust textural fill, have the stitches overlap.

15 **To finish your design in the hoop, see page 146.**

Desert Arches

SKILL LEVEL: BEGINNER

The Delicate Arch in Utah is another bucket-list trip, and one I'm going to be able to cross off soon! For this project, I was inspired by the colors and textures of rock faces. Have fun using different stitches to create textural rocks.

Here's what you'll need to create this design:

- Pattern (page 150)
- 5" (12.7cm) wood embroidery hoop
- Cotton fabric (I used: Desert Curves in Stucco Cream by FIGO Fabrics = pink; Purple Tie
- Dye from JOANN Fabric and Craft – purple)
- #5 embroidery needle
- DMC colors: 301, 400, 435, C436, 918, 920, 975, 977, 3776, 3826, 3856, 3857, 3858, and 3862
- Scissors
- Pencil or erasable pen
- Transfer paper (optional)

ILLUSTRATED STITCH GUIDE

This diagram shows what colors and stitches will be used within this design. Please pay special attention to the number key, which will be referenced in the instructions. Follow the instructions for the layer order, details, and tips on each section.

For detailed instructions on how to create each stitch, see the Stitch Glossary starting on page 20.

1 = DMC 3856 + Back Stitch

2 = DMC 977 + Chain Stitch

3 = DMC 435 + Satin Stitch

4 = DMC 3826 + Back Stitch

5 = DMC 3776 + Satin Stitch

6 = DMC 975 + Satin Stitch

7 = DMC C436 + Long and Short Satin Stitch

8 – DMC 3862 + Satin Stitch

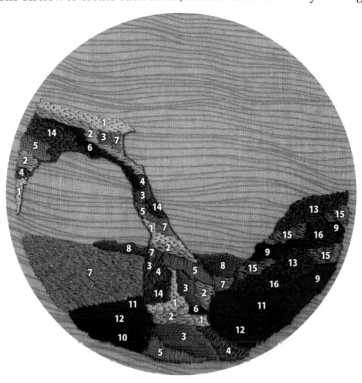

9 = DMC 400 + Satin Stitch

10 = DMC 3857 + Back Stitch

11 = DMC 3858 + Satin Stitch

12 = DMC 918 + Satin Stitch

13 = DMC 920 + Seed Stitch

14 = DMC 301 + Seed Stitch

15 = DMC 3776 + Chain Stitch

16 = DMC 975 + Back Stitch

The lines of this fabric make this scene feel serene.
Add more energy with a tie-dye or other print!

1 **Four sections labeled 1 in number key.**
3 strands of DMC 3856 + Back Stitch. Fill in with horizontal rows.

2 **Four sections labeled 4 in number key.**
3 strands of DMC 3826 + Back Stitch. Fill in with vertical stitches.

3 **One section labeled 10 in number key.**
3 strands of DMC 3857 + Back Stitch. Fill in with horizontal rows.

4 **Two sections labeled 16 in number key.**
3 strands of DMC 975 + Back Stitch. Fill in with horizontal rows.

5 **Four sections labeled 2 in number key.**
3 strands of DMC 977 + Chain Stitch. Fill in with horizontal rows.

6 **Four sections labeled 15 in number key.**
3 strands of DMC 3776 + Chain Stitch. Fill in with horizontal rows.

7 **Two sections labeled 13 in number key.**
3 strands of DMC 920 + Seed Stitch. These sections should be densely filled, with the stitches overlapping one another.

8 **Three sections labeled 14 in number key.** 3 strands of DMC 301 + Seed Stitch. These sections should be densely filled.

9 **Five sections labeled 3 in number key.** 3 strands of DMC 435 + Satin Stitch. Fill in with diagonal stitches.

10 **Four sections labeled 5 in number key.** 3 strands of DMC 3776 + Satin Stitch. Fill in with diagonal stitches.

11 **Two sections labeled 6 in number key.** 3 strands of DMC 975 + Satin Stitch. Fill in with diagonal stitches.

12 **Two sections labeled 8 in number key.** 3 strands of DMC 3862 + Satin Stitch. Fill in with diagonal stitches.

13 **Three sections labeled 9 in number key.** 3 strands of DMC 400 + Satin Stitch. Fill in with diagonal stitches.

14 **Two sections labeled 12 in number key.** 3 strands of DMC 918 + Satin Stitch. Fill in with diagonal stitches.

15 **Two sections labeled 11 in number key.** 3 strands of DMC 3858 + Satin Stitch. Fill in with diagonal stitches.

16 **Three sections labeled 7 in number key.** 3 strands of DMC C436 + Long and Short Satin Stitch.

17 **Rock arch outline.** 1 strand of DMC 3862 + Stem Stitch. This thin outline helps define the arch from the background.

18 To finish your design in the hoop, see page 146.

Purple Mountains Majesty

SKILL LEVEL: BEGINNER

I vividly remember driving back to college one summer
and seeing the landscape change from sagebrush to wheat fields.
I love seeing the vibrant differences that even a short road trip can offer.

Here's what you'll need to create this design:

- Pattern (page 151)
- 4" (10.2cm) wood embroidery hoop
- Cotton fabric (I used: Packed Pinecones Natural by Robert

- Kaufman = neutral; Stars Aligned Treat by Art Gallery Fabrics® = purple)
- #5 embroidery needle

- DMC colors: Blanc, 29, 30, 224, 581, 680, 730, 783, and 832
- Scissors
- Pencil or erasable pen
- Transfer paper (optional)

ILLUSTRATED STITCH GUIDE

This diagram shows what colors and stitches will be used within this design. Follow the instructions for the layer order, details, and tips on each section.

For detailed instructions on how to create each stitch, see the Stitch Glossary starting on page 20.

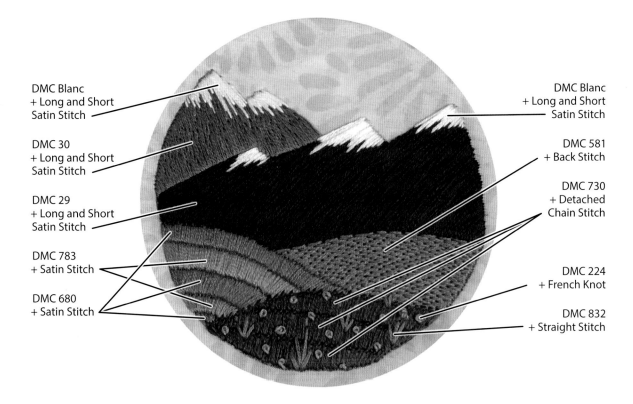

DMC Blanc
+ Long and Short
Satin Stitch

DMC 30
+ Long and Short
Satin Stitch

DMC 29
+ Long and Short
Satin Stitch

DMC 783
+ Satin Stitch

DMC 680
+ Satin Stitch

DMC Blanc
+ Long and Short
Satin Stitch

DMC 581
+ Back Stitch

DMC 730
+ Detached
Chain Stitch

DMC 224
+ French Knot

DMC 832
+ Straight Stitch

The print for this piece could be seen as sun rays or flowers, both of which match the scene.

INSTRUCTIONS

1 **Top-left mountains.** 3 strands of DMC 30 + Long and Short Satin Stitch. Make sure your stitches are very close together; they can overlap to achieve a flat, solid fill of color. Use the angled side of the mountain as a guide to stitch on the diagonal. This will help keep the steep feel of the mountain and make it easier to blend rows of stitches together.

2 **Snowcaps.** 3 strands of DMC Blanc + Long and Short Satin Stitch. Unlike the mountains, don't overlap your rows of the long and short satin stitch.

3 **Bottom-right mountains.** 3 strands of DMC 29 + Long and Short Satin Stitch. Stitch this layer at an opposite angle to the previous mountain, following the angle of the mountainside.

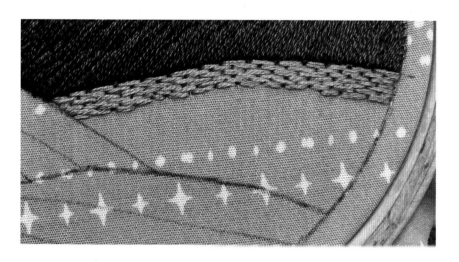

4 **Grass hill.** 3 strands of DMC 581 + Back Stitch. The rows of back stitch should be stitched horizontally across the section. Offsetting each row of back stitch, like bricks, helps the rows blend together.

5 **Top wheat field.** 3 strands of DMC 680 + Satin Stitch.

6 **Top-middle wheat field.** 3 strands of DMC 783 + Satin Stitch.

7 **Bottom three layers of wheat field.** Continuing with the satin stitch, alternate row colors from steps 5–6 to fill in the rest.

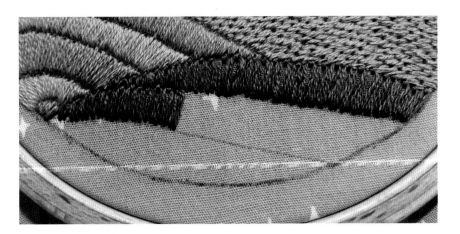

8 **Meadow.** 3 strands of DMC 730 + Detached Chain Stitch. Fill in all three rows of this layer. The detached chain stitch should be stitched on the vertical, sewing horizontally across the section.

9 **Shrubs.** 3 strands of DMC 832 + Straight Stitch. These can be added wherever you like. Each shrub is made of 2–4 straight stitches that connect at the center base.

10 **Flowers.** 3 strands of DMC 224 + French Knot. Again, these can be added wherever you like.

11 **To finish your design in the hoop, see page 146.**

A Walk Among the Wildflowers

SKILL LEVEL: INTERMEDIATE

One of my favorite things about summer is wildflowers. I love seeing them pop in unexpected places and in vibrant colors.

Here's what you'll need to create this design:

- Pattern (page 151)
- 5" x 7½" (12.7 x 19cm) oval wood embroidery hoop
- Cotton fabric (I used Mud Cloth in Flamingo by Gingiber for
- Moda Fabrics and Mint Metallic from JOANN Fabric and Craft)
- #5 embroidery needle
- DMC colors: 22, 320, 322, 351, 368, 501, 722, 729, 745, 900, 3047, 3340, 3687, 3824, 3834, and 3836
- Scissors
- Pencil or erasable pen
- Transfer paper (optional)

ILLUSTRATED STITCH GUIDE

This diagram shows what colors and stitches will be used within this design. Follow the instructions for the layer order, details, and tips on each section.

For detailed instructions on how to create each stitch, see the Stitch Glossary starting on page 20.

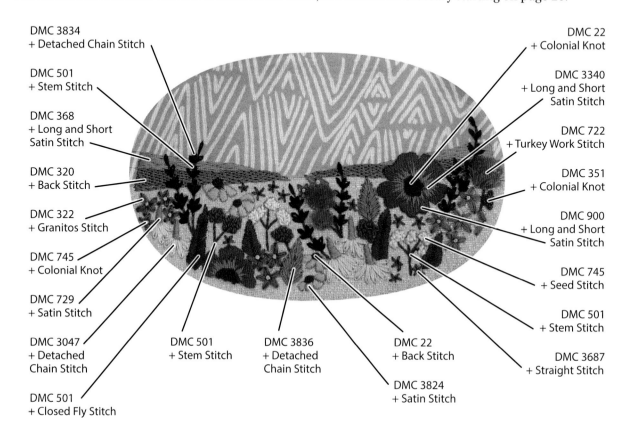

DMC 3834
+ Detached Chain Stitch

DMC 501
+ Stem Stitch

DMC 368
+ Long and Short
Satin Stitch

DMC 320
+ Back Stitch

DMC 322
+ Granitos Stitch

DMC 745
+ Colonial Knot

DMC 729
+ Satin Stitch

DMC 3047
+ Detached
Chain Stitch

DMC 501
+ Closed Fly Stitch

DMC 501
+ Stem Stitch

DMC 3836
+ Detached
Chain Stitch

DMC 22
+ Back Stitch

DMC 3824
+ Satin Stitch

DMC 22
+ Colonial Knot

DMC 3340
+ Long and Short
Satin Stitch

DMC 722
+ Turkey Work Stitch

DMC 351
+ Colonial Knot

DMC 900
+ Long and Short
Satin Stitch

DMC 745
+ Seed Stitch

DMC 501
+ Stem Stitch

DMC 3687
+ Straight Stitch

Layer two (or more!) pieces of fabric to add even more texture and color.

1 **Attach the bottom fabric to the background fabric.** Use the running stitch with any color and number of strands. Once the two fabrics are attached, place the fabric in the hoop and transfer the design.

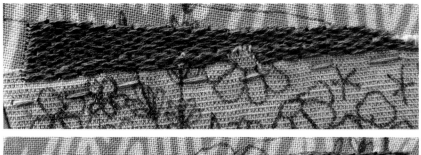

2 **Bottom mountains.** 3 strands of DMC 320 + Back Stitch. This layer is split into two sections on the left and right. These stitches should be made horizontally in rows, offsetting one another like a brick wall. Be sure to stitch over the top raw edge of the bottom fabric and around any flowers that overlap.

3 **Gently pull out the running stitch that held the two fabrics together.**

4 **Top mountains.** 3 strands of DMC 368 + Long and Short Satin Stitch. These stitches should be made horizontally.

5 **Plant stems.** 3 strands of DMC 501 + Stem Stitch.

6 **Leaves.** 3 strands of DMC 501 + Closed Fly Stitch. Start at the top of the leaf and stitch toward the base. These stitches should be very close together to fill in the space.

7 **Centers of cone flowers.** 4 strands of DMC 729 + Satin Stitch. These stitches should be made horizontally.

8 **Petals of cone flowers.** 4 strands of DMC 3047 + Detached Chain Stitch. Fill in the center of the petal with a straight stitch. Petals should start at the base of the cone and be stitched outward.

9 **Lavender flowers.** 3 strands of DMC 3834 + Detached Chain Stitch. Fill in the center of the petal with a straight stitch. Each detached chain stitch should start at the base of the stem. Each group of stitches should fan out around the stem.

10 **Forget-me-not flowers.** 3 strands of DMC 322 + Granitos Stitch. Each petal should be an individual granitos stitch.

11 **Centers of forget-me-not flowers.** 3 strands of DMC 745 + Colonial Knot.

12 **Flower bud bunches.** 6 strands of DMC 351 + Colonial Knot. Each dot will be a colonial knot.

13 **Amaranth.** 3 strands of DMC 3836 + Detached Chain Stitch. Start at the top of the amaranth and work your way down the centerline, keeping the stitches at a diagonal. Then add more detached chain stitches along the centerline, covering the bottom of all the diagonal stitches. Each of these stitches will also overlap at the bottom along the centerline.

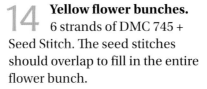

14 **Yellow flower bunches.** 6 strands of DMC 745 + Seed Stitch. The seed stitches should overlap to fill in the entire flower bunch.

15 **Star flowers.** 6 strands of DMC 3687 + Straight Stitch. Each petal of the flower is one straight stitch, with the stitches meeting at a center point.

16 **Petals of daisy flowers.** 3 strands of DMC 3824 + Satin Stitch. Each individual petal should be filled in on the diagonal with each petal's stitches made in the opposite direction.

17 **Centers of daisy flowers.** 3 strands of DMC 22 + Back Stitch. Offset the different rows like bricks in a wall. This will create an even fill and disguise where the stitches connect.

18 **Inner petals of poppy flowers.** 3 strands of DMC 3340 + Long and Short Satin Stitch. Stitches should start at the edge of the poppy center and fan out toward the middle of the poppy petals.

19 **Outer petals of poppy flowers.** 3 strands of DMC 900 + Long and Short Satin Stitch. Start at the outside edge of the petals and stitch toward the section that is filled. Stitches should slightly overlap so that where they connect blends together.

20 **Centers of poppy flowers.** 6 strands of DMC 22 + Colonial Knot. These knots should overlap to create a densely filed texture.

21 **Orange fluff-ball flowers.** 6 strands of DMC 722 + Turkey Work Stitch. Stitches should be made in horizontal rows, starting and the top of circle and adding rows below to fill in the shape. The more turkey work stitches added, the fluffier the fluff ball will be. When cutting down the turkey work, trim small portions at a time. Remember, you can always trim more—you can't trim less!

22 **To finish your design in the hoop, see page 146.**

Scenic Lookout

SKILL LEVEL: INTERMEDIATE

A few years ago, I road-tripped to San Francisco for a craft show
and took the Pacific Coast Scenic Byway. The many beautiful views had me
making multiple stops to take photos along the way.

Here's what you'll need to create this design:

- Pattern (page 152)
- 5" (12.7cm) wood embroidery hoop
- Cotton fabric (I used Rose Garden Ice Dyed Fabric by MCreativeJ)
- #5 embroidery needle
- DMC colors: 520, 838, 926, 927, 928, 935, 936, 3011, 3756, 3808, and 3809
- Scissors
- Pencil or erasable pen
- Transfer paper (optional)

ILLUSTRATED STITCH GUIDE

This diagram shows what colors and stitches will be used within this design. Follow the instructions for the layer order, details, and tips on each section.

For detailed instructions on how to create each stitch, see the Stitch Glossary starting on page 20.

DMC 3809 + Long and Short Satin Stitch

DMC 3756 + Long and Short Satin Stitch

DMC 935 + Detached Buttonhole Stitch

DMC 936 + Detached Buttonhole Stitch

DMC 838 + Split Back Stitch & Back Stitch

DMC 928 + Seed Stitch

DMC 927 + Seed Stitch

DMC 3756 + Satin Stitch

DMC 926 + Seed Stitch

DMC 520 + Split Back Stitch

DMC 3808 + Long and Short Satin Stitch

DMC 935 + Back Stitch

DMC 3011 + Chain Stitch

Hand-dyed fabric is a great way to recreate the natural sky at sunset.

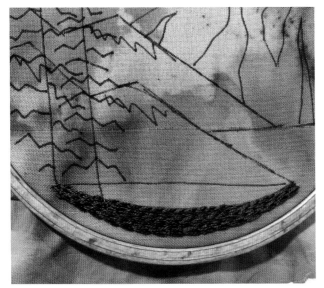

1 **Bottom landscape.** 3 strands of DMC 3011 + Chain Stitch. These chain stitches should be made from one side to the other, following the bottom of the pattern.

2 **Middle landscape.** 3 strands of DMC 935 + Back Stitch. These stitches should be made horizontally in rows, with each row offset like bricks. Be sure to leave a space and not stitch over the tree trunks that overlap this landscape layer.

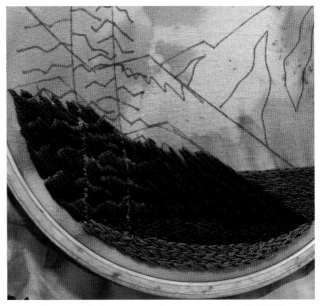

3 **Top-right landscape.** 3 strands of DMC 520 + Split Back Stitch. Use the top line of the section as a guide for creating the horizontal stitch lines that will fill in the shape.

4 **Bottom-left mountains.** 3 strands of DMC 3808 + Long and Short Satin Stitch. Fill in with stitches going at a downward angle, following the angle of the mountain. Use 3–4 rows of stitches to fill in this section. Be sure to stitch around the tree trunks and branches so you can see where to stitch them later.

5 **Snowcaps on bottom-left mountains.** 3 strands of DMC 3756 + Long and Short Satin Stitch. Stitch around the tree branches.

6 **Middle-left mountains.** 3 strands of DMC 3809 + Long and Short Satin Stitch. Follow the slant of the mountain to angle the stitches. Stitch around the tree branches.

7 **Snowcap on bottom-left mountains.** 3 strands of DMC 3756 + Long and Short Satin Stitch.

8 **Snowdrifts on top-right mountains.** 3 strands of DMC 3756 + Satin Stitch. Stitching these sections on the diagonal will make it easier to fill in the zigzag shapes.

9 **Bottom of top-right mountains.** 4 strands of DMC 926 + Seed Stitch. These seed stitches should overlap to create a dense textural fill within the shape.

10 **Middle of top-right mountains.** 4 strands of DMC 927 + Seed Stitch.

11 **Top of top-right mountains.** 4 strands of DMC 928 + Seed Stitch.

12 **Trees.** 6 strands of DMC 838 + Split Back Stitch for the trunks. 6 strands of DMC 838 + Back Stitch for the branches.

13 **Greenery on right tree.** 6 strands of DMC 936 + Detached Buttonhole Stitch. Use the tree branches as the base for your stitch. When creating the detached buttonhole stitch, bring the needle up in the hole that makes the end of the tree branch. Slide the needle under the tree branch, toward the base of the tree trunk. Start at the top of the tree and work downward.

14 **Greenery on left tree.** 6 strands of DMC 935 + Detached Buttonhole Stitch.

15 **To finish your design in the hoop, see page 146.**

Desert Oasis

SKILL LEVEL: INTERMEDIATE

When thinking about visits to my mother-in-law in Arizona,
I often reflect on the views from her neighborhood. With just a few steps
outside, you can see gorgeous red rock hills covered in cacti.

Here's what you'll need to create this design:

- Pattern (page 152)
- 5" (12.7cm) wood embroidery hoop
- Cotton fabric (I used: Moonscape in Orchid by Dear Stella =

purple; FUN-C8224 by Timeless Treasures Fabrics = orange)
- DMC colors: 165, 166, 730, 738, 746, 918, 922, 924, 3771, and 3815

- #5 embroidery needle
- Scissors
- Pencil or erasable pen
- Transfer paper (optional)

ILLUSTRATED STITCH GUIDE

This diagram shows what colors and stitches will be used within this design. Follow the instructions for the layer order, details, and tips on each section.

For detailed instructions on how to create each stitch, see the Stitch Glossary starting on page 20.

DMC 165
+ Reverse
Chain Stitch

DMC 166
+ Reverse
Chain Stitch

DMC 924
+ Satin Stitch

DMC 3815
+ Satin Stitch

DMC 746
+ Back Stitch

DMC 918
+ Seed Stitch

DMC 3771
+ French Knot

DMC 738
+ Connected
Fly Stitch

DMC 730
+ Satin Stitch

DMC 922
+ Back Stitch

Purple fabric turns this into a nighttime scene, while a warm color indicates day.

1 **Sun.** 3 strands of DMC 746 + Back Stitch. Create a back stitch in the center of the sun, then stitch in a circle around it toward the outer edge.

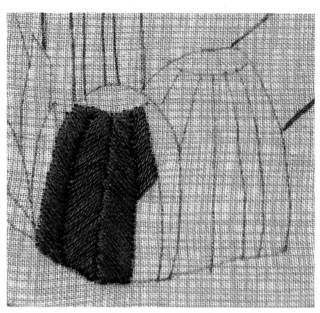

2 **Barrel cacti.** 3 strands of DMC 730 + Satin Stitch. Stitch each section of the cactus at opposing angles.

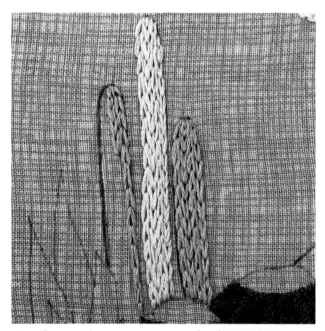

3 **Organ pipe cactus.** 4 strands of DMC 165 + Reverse Chain Stitch for the middle. Fill in with vertical stitches. 4 strands of DMC 166 + Reverse Chain Stitch for the right and left. Fill in with vertical stitches.

4 **Middle agave leaves.** 3 strands of DMC 924 + Satin Stitch. Stitch these leaves on the diagonal to fill in the shape easier.

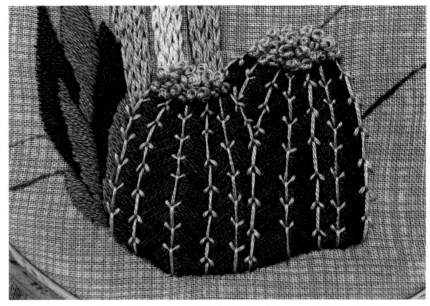

5 **Bottom and top agave leaves.** 3 strands of DMC 3815 + Satin Stitch. These leaves will also be stitched on the diagonal.

6 **Cactus spines.** 2 strands of DMC 738 + Connected Fly Stitch. Add cactus spines between where the satin stitches meet on the barrel cacti.

7 **Blooms on the barrel cacti.** 6 strands of DMC 3771 + French Knot. Differ the number of times you wrap the thread around the needle to make the knots different sizes.

8 **Bottom landscape.** 3 strands of DMC 922 + Back Stitch. Start at the top of the section and create horizontal rows that are stacked like bricks.

9 **Top landscape.** 3 strands of DMC 918 + Seed Stitch. This layer should be densely filled, with the stitches overlapping one another.

10 **To finish your design in the hoop, see page 146.**

A Pacific Northwest Spring

SKILL LEVEL: INTERMEDIATE

A couple times a year, my husband and I drive up to visit my father-in-law in the Mount Vernon area of Washington. Spring is my favorite time to make this trip because the tulips are in bloom and the mountains look vibrant.

Here's what you'll need to create this design:

- Pattern (page 153)
- 8" x 5" (20.3 x 12.7cm) oval wood embroidery hoop
- Cotton fabric (I used Paper Cuts by Rashida Coleman for Cotton + Steel)
- #5 embroidery needle
- DMC colors: 309, 469, 520, 775, 930, 931, 988, 3047, 3341, 3825, 3865
- Scissors
- Pencil or erasable pen
- Transfer paper (optional)

ILLUSTRATED STITCH GUIDE

This diagram shows what colors and stitches will be used within this design. Follow the instructions for the layer order, details, and tips on each section.

For detailed instructions on how to create each stitch, see the Stitch Glossary starting on page 20.

DMC 3047
+ Satin Stitch &
Split Back Stitch

DMC 3865
+ Satin Stitch

DMC 931
+ Satin Stitch

DMC 520
+ Split Back Stitch

DMC 3825
+ Danish Knot

DMC 930
+ Satin Stitch

DMC 775
+ Satin Stitch

DMC 988
+ Back Stitch

DMC 469
+ Seed Stitch

DMC 309 & 3341
+ Tulip Stitch

The textural flower field at the base mirrors the bold print of the background fabric at the top.

INSTRUCTIONS

1 **Snowcap on mountain.** 3 strands of DMC 3865 + Satin Stitch. Use the angle of the mountain to define the slant of the stitches.

2 **Top layer of mountain.** 3 strands of DMC 930 + Satin Stitch. Continue to use the slant of the mountainside to determine the angle of the stitches.

3 **Top snowdrifts on mountain.** 3 strands of DMC 3865 + Satin Stitch.

4 **Middle layer of mountain.** 3 strands of DMC 931 + Satin Stitch.

5 **Bottom snowdrifts on mountain.** 3 strands of DMC 3865 + Satin Stitch.

6 **Bottom layer of mountain.** 3 strands of DMC 775 + Satin Stitch.

7 **Right and left meadow sections.** 3 strands of DMC 988 + Back Stitch. These back stitches should be made in horizontal rows following the line of the landscape layer. Offset each row of stitches like bricks in a wall.

8 **Middle meadow section.** 3 strands of DMC 520 + Split Back Stitch. These stitches will also be made horizontally, following the line of the landscape layer.

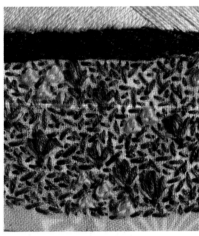

9 **Triangle sections in field.** 6 strands of 3825 + Danish Knot. Each triangle in the pattern is a Danish knot.

10 **Flowers in field.** 4 strands of DMC 309 & 4 strands of DMC 3341 + Tulip Stitch. Thread the colors in separate needles. DMC 309 will be used for the loop and inner *V*. DMC 3341 will be used for the outer *V* and fill the center loop.

11 **Grass.** 3 strands of DMC 469 + Seed Stitch. These stitches should be like sprinkles, filling in the section while still leaving space between each stitch.

12 **Sun.** 3 strands of DMC 3047 + Satin Stitch to fill in the circle. 3 strands of DMC 3047 + Split Back Stitch to outline the circle. Use small stitches while going around the outline to help the stitches hug the curve. This will also help even out the edges of the satin stitches.

13 **To finish your design in the hoop, see page 146.**

Mountain Brook

SKILL LEVEL: INTERMEDIATE

I will admit, I'm not big on tent camping (I'm a hotel kind of girl).
On one of my rare tent camping forays, we stayed next to a gorgeous mountain
stream. This project was inspired by that summer memory.

Here's what you'll need to create this design:

- Pattern (page 153)
- 6" (15.2cm) wood embroidery hoop
- Cotton fabric (I used: Prisma Dyes Artisan Batik Lavender by Robert Kaufman = purple; Spark

- Butterscotch by Melody Miller for Ruby Star Society = gold)
- #5 embroidery needle
- DMC colors: 17, 21, 26, 501, 503, 535, 580, 731, 832, 3345, 3750, 3841, and 4150

- Scissors
- Pencil or erasable pen
- Transfer paper (optional)

ILLUSTRATED STITCH GUIDE

This diagram shows what colors and stitches will be used within this design. Follow the instructions for the layer order, details, and tips on each section.

For detailed instructions on how to create each stitch, see the Stitch Glossary starting on page 20.

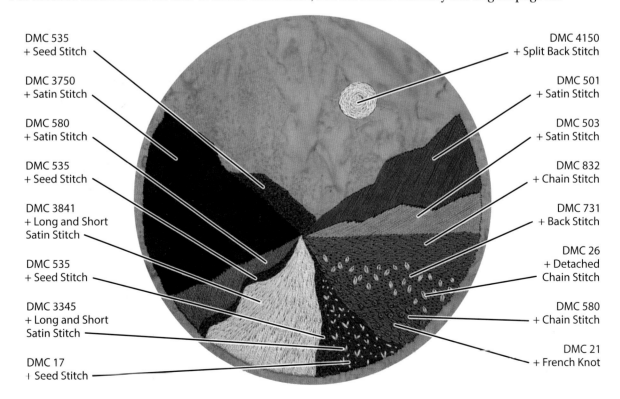

DMC 535 + Seed Stitch

DMC 3750 + Satin Stitch

DMC 580 + Satin Stitch

DMC 535 + Seed Stitch

DMC 3841 + Long and Short Satin Stitch

DMC 535 + Seed Stitch

DMC 3345 + Long and Short Satin Stitch

DMC 17 + Seed Stitch

DMC 4150 + Split Back Stitch

DMC 501 + Satin Stitch

DMC 503 + Satin Stitch

DMC 832 + Chain Stitch

DMC 731 + Back Stitch

DMC 26 + Detached Chain Stitch

DMC 580 + Chain Stitch

DMC 21 + French Knot

There are many ways to indicate a night sky without using black or blue. The left fabric includes sweet little stars while the right is filled with clouds.

1 **Sun.** 3 strands of DMC 4150 + Split Back Stitch. Start at the outer edge of the circle and work your way in.

2 **Top-right mountain.** 3 strands of DMC 501 + Satin Stitch. Use the edge of the mountain as a guide for how to angle your satin stitches.

3 **Bottom-right mountain.** 3 strands of DMC 503 + Satin Stitch. Use the edge of the mountain as a guide for how to angle the satin stitches.

4 **Middle mountain.** 3 strands of DMC 535 + Seed Stitch.

5 **Left mountain.** 3 strands of DMC 3750 + Satin Stitch. Each section of the mountain is filled in with satin stitch. Stitch each section of the mountain in a different direction, which will add depth and dimension to the mountainside.

6 **Left field.** 3 strands of DMC 580 + Satin Stitch. Keep these stitches at an upward diagonal to help with the perspective of this piece.

7 **Rocks.** 3 strands of DMC 535 + Seed Stitch. There is a section on either side of the water.

8 **Water.** 3 strands of DMC 3841 + Long and Short Satin Stitch. Start at the narrowest point of the brook and stitch out toward the wider section.

9 **Top-right field.** 3 strands of DMC 832 + Chain Stitch. These stitches should be made across the section horizontally.

10 **Top-middle-right field.** 3 strands of DMC 731 + Back Stitch. The rows of back stitch should be created horizontally across the section. Offset each row of back stitches, like bricks, to help the rows blend together.

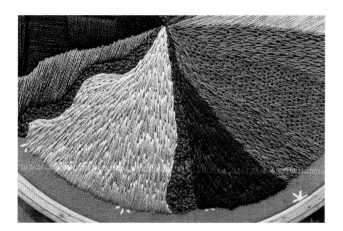

11 **Bottom-middle-right field.** 3 strands of DMC 580 + Chain Stitch.

12 **Bottom-right field.** 3 strands of DMC 3345 + Long and Short Satin Stitch. Use the edge of the rocks as a guide for how to angle your rows.

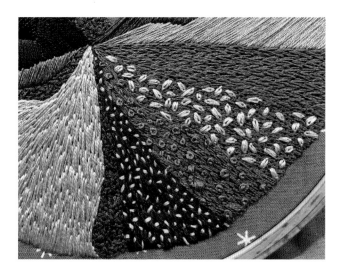

13 **Flowers on top-middle-right field.** 3 strands of DMC 26 + Detached Chain Stitch. These can be sprinkled wherever you'd like.

14 **Flowers on bottom-middle-right field.** 3 strands of DMC 21 + French Knot. These can be sprinkled wherever you'd like.

15 **Flowers on bottom-right field.** 3 strands of DMC 17 + Seed Stitch. These can be sprinkled wherever you'd like.

16 **To finish your design in the hoop, see page 146.**

From the Heartland

Have you ever made a cross-country road trip? During the summer of 2022, I drove from Seattle to Chicago and back. There were many amazing views along the way, but one thing that struck me was how the landscape flattened out after Montana. This pattern is inspired by the rolling hills and crop fields I saw along my trip.

Here's what you'll need to create this design:

- Pattern (page 154)
- 8" (20.3cm) square wood embroidery hoop
- Cotton fabric (I used Add It Up in Rust by Alexia Abegg for Ruby Star Society)

- #5 embroidery needle
- DMC colors: 422, 611, 632, 680, 729, 730, 732, 830, 841, 3045, 3051, 3364, and 3790

- Scissors
- Erasable pen
- Transfer paper

ILLUSTRATED STITCH GUIDE

This diagram shows what colors and stitches will be used within this design. Follow the instructions for the layer order, details, and tips on each section.

For detailed instructions on how to create each stitch, see the Stitch Glossary starting on page 20.

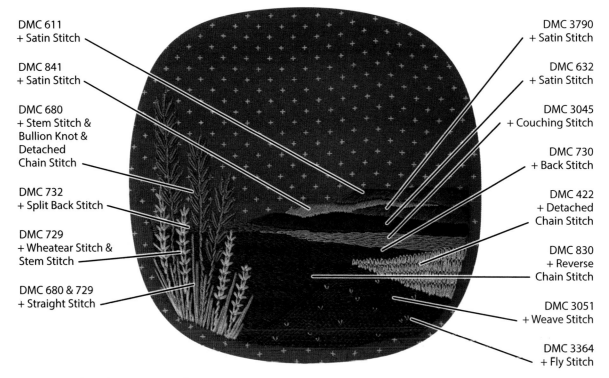

DMC 611
+ Satin Stitch

DMC 841
+ Satin Stitch

DMC 680
+ Stem Stitch &
Bullion Knot &
Detached
Chain Stitch

DMC 732
+ Split Back Stitch

DMC 729
+ Wheatear Stitch &
Stem Stitch

DMC 680 & 729
+ Straight Stitch

DMC 3790
+ Satin Stitch

DMC 632
+ Satin Stitch

DMC 3045
+ Couching Stitch

DMC 730
+ Back Stitch

DMC 422
+ Detached
Chain Stitch

DMC 830
+ Reverse
Chain Stitch

DMC 3051
+ Weave Stitch

DMC 3364
+ Fly Stitch

This fabric has a simple, homey feeling that matches perfectly with the theme of the embroidery design.

1 **Bottom-right landscape.** 3 strands of DMC 3051 + Weave Stitch. The first row of stitches should follow the angle of the shape.

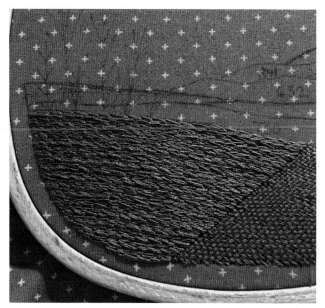

2 **Bottom-left landscape.** 3 strands of DMC 830 + Reverse Chain Stitch. These stitches should be made in horizontal rows. Use the top of the landscape section as a guide to start the first row.

3 **Middle landscape.** 3 strands of DMC 730 + Back Stitch. These stitches should be created in horizontal rows. When filling this section, offset each row of back stitches like bricks to disguise where the stitches connect.

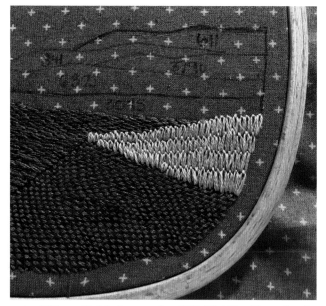

4 **Wheat field.** 3 strands of DMC 422 + Detached Chain Stitch. These stitches are made vertically. Start at the top of the section and fill the rows below. Rows of vertical stitches will fill the section horizontally. Each row will slightly overlap each other.

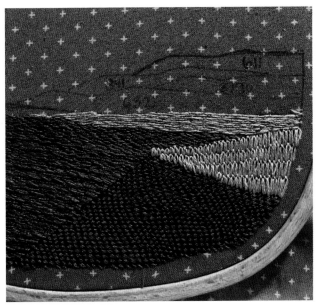

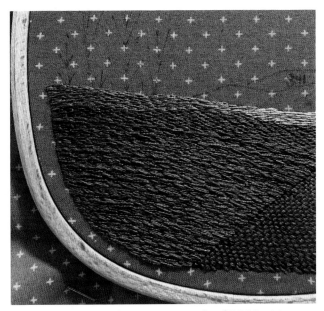

5 **Top-right landscape.** 4x2 strands of DMC 3045 + Couching Stitch. The straight line is made with 4 strands of thread; the 2 strands are used to tack the thread down to the fabric. These stitches should be made horizontally across the shape.

6 **Top-left landscape.** 3 strands of DMC 732 + Split Back Stitch. This layer is stitched in horizontal rows.

7 **Bottom layer of mountain.** 3 strands of DMC 632 + Satin Stitch. These stitches should be made at a downward angle, using the slanted side of the landscape layer as a guide.

8 **Middle-right layer of mountain.** 3 strands of DMC 3790 + Satin Stitch. Stitch at a downward angle, using the slanted side of the landscape layer as a guide.

9 **Middle-left layer of mountain.** 3 strands of DMC 841 + Satin Stitch. Stitch at a downward angle, using the slanted side of the landscape layer as a guide.

10 **Top layer of mountain.** 3 strands of DMC 611 + Satin Stitch. Stitch at a downward angle, using the slanted side of the landscape layer as a guide.

11 **Grass blades.** 2 strands of DMC 3364 + Fly Stitch. Add small *V*s in the bottom-right landscape.

12 **Determine your method for making the wheat stalk stitches.** Because these are on top of the landscape, you can either eyeball the wheat stalks or use a transfer paper. If using a transfer paper, trace the design onto the paper, then stick it on top of the landscape layers before continuing.

13 **Short wheat stalk grains.** 6 strands of DMC 729 + Wheatear Stitch to create the top sections. Use the eye of the needle instead of the point to slide under the strands of thread; this prevents the needle from getting caught. Don't tug the thread tight to the fabric, otherwise it will be hard to slide the needle underneath without catching the stitches below.

14 **Short wheat stalk stems.** 6 strands of DMC 729 + Stem Stitch.

15 **Tall wheat stalk stems.** 6 strands of DMC 680 + Stem Stitch.

16 **Tall wheat stalk grains.** 3 strands of DMC 680 + Bullion Knot to make the inner grain. The bullion knot should cover about two-thirds the length of each diagonal line connecting to the stems of the wheat stalk. 3 strands of DMC 680 + Detached Chain Stitch to surround the bullion knot. Extend the short tacking stitch at the top of the detached chain stitch to create the top of the wheat stalk.

17 **Wheat leaves.** 2 strands of DMC 680 & 2 strands of DMC 729 + Straight Stitch. Create straight lines around the wheat stalks to fill in the foreground. These stitches should vary in length and angle.

18 **To finish your design in the hoop, see page 146.**

It Was All a Mirage

SKILL LEVEL: ADVANCED

One of the many things I love about visiting Arizona is that, even on short walks, you can see so many varieties of cacti growing among the hills.

Here's what you'll need to create this design:

- Pattern (page 154)
- 6" (15.2cm) wood embroidery hoop
- Cotton fabric (I used: Rose from Kona Cotton = pink; Island

- Batik in Cantaloupe Dots from Neptune's Friends = orange)
- #5 embroidery needle
- DMC colors: 350, 422, 580, 676, 830, 904, 934, 3341, 3771, 3817, 3823, 3830, 3848, and 3858

- Scissors
- Pencil or erasable pen
- Transfer paper (optional)

ILLUSTRATED STITCH GUIDE

This diagram shows what colors and stitches will be used within this design. Follow the instructions for the layer order, details, and tips on each section.

For detailed instructions on how to create each stitch, see the Stitch Glossary starting on page 20.

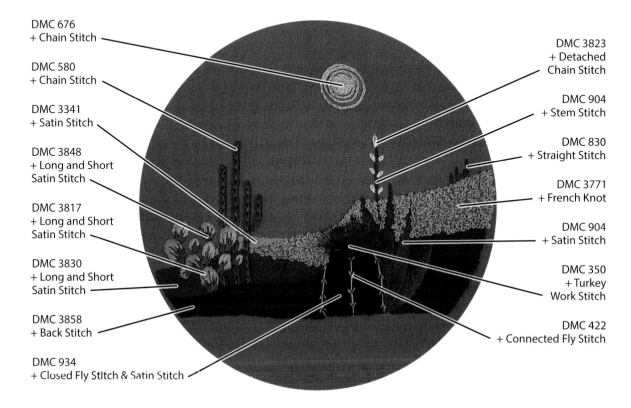

DMC 676 + Chain Stitch

DMC 580 + Chain Stitch

DMC 3341 + Satin Stitch

DMC 3848 + Long and Short Satin Stitch

DMC 3817 + Long and Short Satin Stitch

DMC 3830 + Long and Short Satin Stitch

DMC 3858 + Back Stitch

DMC 934 + Closed Fly Stitch & Satin Stitch

DMC 3823 + Detached Chain Stitch

DMC 904 + Stem Stitch

DMC 830 + Straight Stitch

DMC 3771 + French Knot

DMC 904 + Satin Stitch

DMC 350 + Turkey Work Stitch

DMC 422 + Connected Fly Stitch

Sometimes it's better to pick a plain fabric that complements the design so the colors in your piece can truly shine!

INSTRUCTIONS

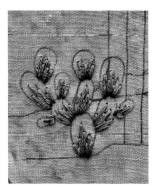

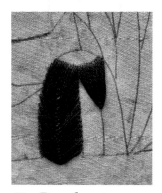

1 **Bottom of prickly pear cactus pads.** 2 strands of DMC 3848 + Long and Short Satin Stitch.

2 **Top of prickly pear cactus pads.** 2 strands of DMC 3817 + Long and Short Satin Stitch. Blend this second color into the first. Start the stitches at the outer edge of the cactus pad then bring the needle down into the top of the long and short stitches, slightly overlapping the colors.

3 **Barrel cactus.** 3 strands of DMC 934 + Closed Fly Stitch. Each stitch fills in two sections of the cactus. The closed fly stitch will also end with a point at the bottom of each cactus section. To fill the cactus in fully, add satin stitches on either side of the closed fly stitch.

4 **Yucca plant leaves.** 3 strands of DMC 904 + Satin Stitch. Stitch each leaf at an opposing angle.

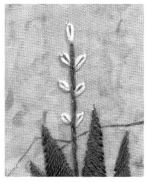

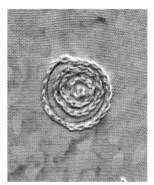

5 **Yucca plant.** 3 strands of DMC 904 + Stem Stitch for the stem. 3 strands of DMC 3823 + Detached Chain Stitch for the flowers. Start each detached chain against the stem line.

6 **Sun.** 3 strands of 676 + Chain Stitch. Start along the outer edge and stitch in a circle toward the center. Make small stitches to keep the circular shape.

7 **Bottom landscape.** 3 strands of DMC 3858 + Back Stitch. Start at the bottom of the layer and create a horizontal row. Each row should be stitched directly above the last and stitches will be offset, like a brick wall, to fill in this section.

9 **Top-left landscape.** 2 strands of DMC 3341 + Satin Stitch. Stitch on the diagonal and around the cacti.

10 **Saguaro cacti.** 6 strands of DMC 580 + Chain Stitch. Each line of the cactus is a single row of chain stitches.

8 **Middle-left landscape.** 2 strands of DMC 3830 + Long and Short Satin Stitch. Create these stitches on a diagonal, making it easier to stitch around the prickly pear cactus and lines for the saguaro cacti.

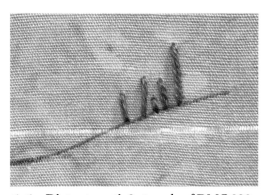

11 **Distant cacti.** 3 strands of DMC 830 + Straight Stitch.

12 **Top-right landscape.** 3 strands of DMC 3771 + French Knot. These should be a dense textural fill. Mix up the number of times the thread is wrapped around the needle to create different sizes of knots.

13 **Barrel cactus spines.** 2 strands of DMC 422 + Connected Fly Stitch. These stitches should be made along the outer edge of the barrel cactus as well as the centerline where the closed fly stitches connect in the center.

14 **Barrel cactus blooms.** 6 strands of DMC 350 + Turkey Work Stitch. Start at the top of the shape and create rows of turkey work, filling in the shape. Once the section is filled in, trim the turkey work to create a fringe.

15 **To finish your design in the hoop, see page 146.**

Tropical Waterfall

SKILL LEVEL: ADVANCED

My two trips to Hawaii were because my husband and I
attended weddings. And I'm so thankful we decided to go. On one of these trips,
we visited a Kauai waterfall that looks similar to this project.

Here's what you'll need to create this design:

- Pattern (page 155)
- 8" x 5" (20.3 x 12.7cm) oval wood embroidery hoop
- Cotton fabric (I used Sky from Kona Cotton)
- #5 embroidery needle
- DMC colors: Blanc, 8, 15, 319, 470, 597, 747, 838, 904, 906, 937, 3345, 3761, 3810, and 4200
- Scissors
- Pencil or erasable pen
- Transfer paper (optional)

ILLUSTRATED STITCH GUIDE

This diagram shows what colors and stitches will be used within this design. Follow the instructions for the layer order, details, and tips on each section.

For detailed instructions on how to create each stitch, see the Stitch Glossary starting on page 20.

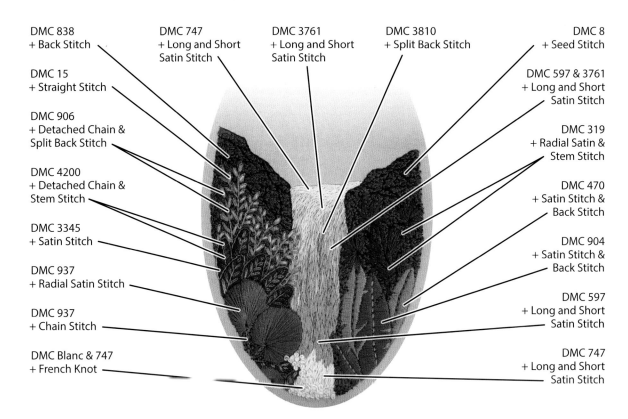

DMC 838
+ Back Stitch

DMC 15
+ Straight Stitch

DMC 906
+ Detached Chain &
Split Back Stitch

DMC 4200
+ Detached Chain &
Stem Stitch

DMC 3345
+ Satin Stitch

DMC 937
+ Radial Satin Stitch

DMC 937
+ Chain Stitch

DMC Blanc & 747
+ French Knot

DMC 747
+ Long and Short
Satin Stitch

DMC 3761
+ Long and Short
Satin Stitch

DMC 3810
+ Split Back Stitch

DMC 8
+ Seed Stitch

DMC 597 & 3761
+ Long and Short
Satin Stitch

DMC 319
+ Radial Satin &
Stem Stitch

DMC 470
+ Satin Stitch &
Back Stitch

DMC 904
+ Satin Stitch &
Back Stitch

DMC 597
+ Long and Short
Satin Stitch

DMC 747
+ Long and Short
Satin Stitch

Having so much blue fabric on top tricks the eye into thinking the waterfall is much longer than it is.

1 **Ruffled fan palm leaves.** 3 strands of DMC 937 + Radial Satin Stitch. Start at the outer edge of the plant and stitch toward the center.

2 **Ruffled fan palm stems.** 3 strands of DMC 937 + Chain Stitch.

3 **Croton plant leaves.** 3 strands of DMC 3345 + Satin Stitch. Start at the outer edge of the leaves and stitch toward the centerline at a 45-degree angle.

4 **Details on croton plant leaves.** 2 strands of DMC 4200 + Detached Chain Stitch to create the loops. Add color details on the front of each leaf around the centerline of the leaves. 2 strands of DMC 4200 + Stem Stitch to outline each leaf and fill in the leaf centerlines. Outlining after filling a shape helps clean up any uneven edges.

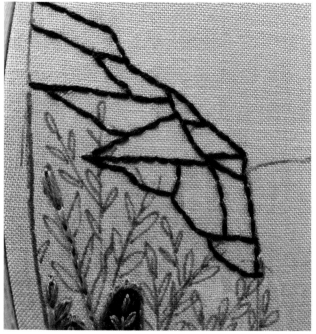

5 **Rock face outline.** 3 strands of DMC 838 + Back Stitch. Stitch on either side of the waterfall.

6 **Ficus branches.** 3 strands of DMC 906 + Split Back Stitch.

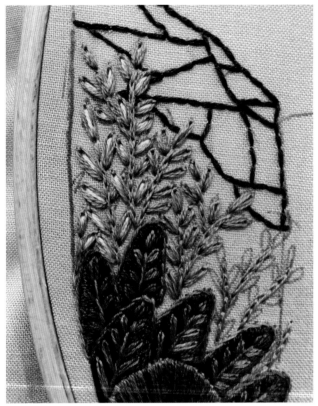

8 **Front banana palm leaves.** 3 strands of DMC 904 + Satin Stitch to make the leaves. Stitch from the outer edge to the centerline, creating horizontal stitches. 3 strands of DMC 470 + Back Stitch to create the center stem line.

7 **Ficus leaves.** 3 strands of DMC 906 + Detached Chain Stitch. One detached chain stitch creates one leaf. 3 strands of DMC 15 + Straight Stitch. Fill in each of the detached chain stitch leaves.

9 **Back banana palm leaves.** 3 strands of DMC 470 + Satin Stitch to make the leaves. Stitch horizontally. 3 strands of DMC 904 + Back Stitch to create the center stem line.

10 **Fan palm stems.** 3 strands of DMC 319 + Stem Stitch.

11 **Fan palm leaves.** 3 strands of DMC 319 + Radial Satin Stitch. Each leaf is composed of three stitches: a long-side stitch, a short middle stitch, and another long-side stitch. Combined, these create a triangle leaf. Cap off each of the outer leaf edges with a short satin stitch.

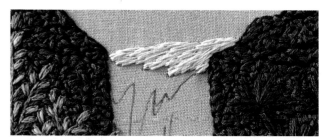

12 **Rock face.** 6 strands of DMC 8 + Seed Stitch. Be sure to stitch in between the plant leaves to get a solid, even fill.

13 **Top layer of waterfall layer.** 3 strands of DMC 747 + Long and Short Satin Stitch. The top section should be stitched on a diagonal, following the angle of the water as it crests over the waterfall edge.

14 **Bottom layer of waterfall.** 3 strands of DMC 747 + Long and Short Satin Stitch. Stitch the lower section vertically to highlight the water cascading downward.

15 **Top-middle layer of waterfall.** 3 strands of DMC 3761 + Long and Short Satin Stitch. Stitch this section at a 335 degree angle to continue the flow of the water over the crest of the waterfall.

16 **Streams.** 3 strands of DMC 3810 + Split Back Stitch. These are lines within the waterfall that will be stitched around.

17 **Middle layer of waterfall.** 2 strands of DMC 3761 & 1 strand of DMC 597 + Long and Short Satin Stitch. Stitch vertically to show the water plunging downward.

18 **Bottom-middle layer of waterfall.** 1 strand of DMC 3761 & 2 strands of DMC 597 + Long and Short Satin Stitch. Use 3 strands of DMC 597 to fill in the base of this section before merging with the bottom layer of the waterfall.

19 **Waterfall spray.** 2 strands DMC Blanc & 1 strand of DMC 747 + French Knot. Vary the wraps on the French knots to add extra texture and depth.

20 **To finish your design in the hoop, see page 146.**

A Walk Along the English Seaside

SKILL LEVEL: ADVANCED

As a child, my dad traveled quite a bit to England for work.
I was fortunate enough to get to visit with my family one summer. While we
saw *a lot* of castles, we also visited a seaside similar to this.

Here's what you'll need to create this design:

- Pattern (page 155)
- 5" (12.7cm) wood embroidery hoop
- Cotton fabric (I used: Yellow Swirl Dot Batik by Robert Kaufman = yellow; The Open

- Road Terrain Overlook Yellow by Bonnie Christine for Art Gallery Fabrics = yellow/white)
- #5 embroidery needle

- DMC colors: 6, 7, 8, 597, 598, 676, 745, 828, 3011, 3012, 3348, 3811, 3823, 3841, and 4150
- Scissors
- Pencil or erasable pen
- Transfer paper (optional)

ILLUSTRATED STITCH GUIDE

This diagram shows what colors and stitches will be used within this design. Follow the instructions for the layer order, details, and tips on each section.

For detailed instructions on how to create each stitch, see the Stitch Glossary starting on page 20

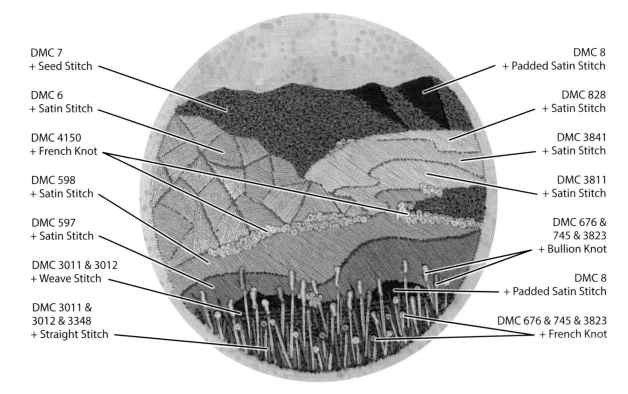

DMC 7 + Seed Stitch

DMC 6 + Satin Stitch

DMC 4150 + French Knot

DMC 598 + Satin Stitch

DMC 597 + Satin Stitch

DMC 3011 & 3012 + Weave Stitch

DMC 3011 & 3012 & 3348 + Straight Stitch

DMC 8 + Padded Satin Stitch

DMC 828 + Satin Stitch

DMC 3841 + Satin Stitch

DMC 3811 + Satin Stitch

DMC 676 & 745 & 3823 + Bullion Knot

DMC 8 + Padded Satin Stitch

DMC 676 & 745 & 3823 + French Knot

A yellow print not only complements the yellow flowers but also makes the blue water pop.

INSTRUCTIONS

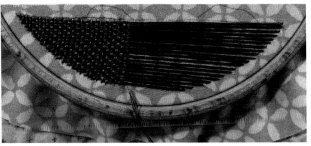

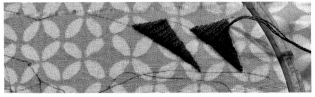

1 **Bottom landscape.** 3 strands of DMC 3011 + Weave Stitch to stitch the horizontal lines. Because you want a solid fill of color in this weave, stitch your rows about a stitch's width apart. Use 3 strands of DMC 3012 to stitch the vertical lines. Weave using the eye of the embroidery needle so as not to split apart the horizontal strands of thread. These stitches should also be very close together to create a compact weave.

2 **Bottom rocks.** 3 strands of DMC 8 + Padded Satin Stitch. The padded satin stitch adds more volume to these sections of the rock face.

3 **Top-right mountain shadows.** 3 strands of DMC 8 + Padded Satin Stitch.

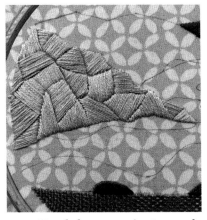

5 **Top-right mountain.** 3 strands of DMC 7 + Seed Stitch. These stitches should overlap and be very compact to completely fill the sections.

6 **Middle-right mountain.** 3 strands of DMC 7 + Seed Stitch.

4 **Top-left mountain.** 3 strands of DMC 6 + Satin Stitch. Each section of this rock face should be stitched in a different direction. This helps the sections stand out, adds depth, and creates what looks like a rock surface.

7 **Top water.** 3 strands of DMC 828 + Satin Stitch. Stitches should be created at diagonal.

8 **Top-middle water.** 3 strands of DMC 3841 + Satin Stitch. This is stitched at a similar angle to keep the perspective of water flowing in the same direction.

9 **Middle water.** 3 strands of DMC 3811 + Satin Stitch.

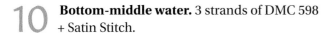

10 **Bottom-middle water.** 3 strands of DMC 598 + Satin Stitch.

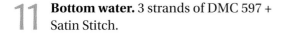

11 **Bottom water.** 3 strands of DMC 597 + Satin Stitch.

12 **Water foam.** 2 strands of DMC 4150 + French Knot. Vary the number of times the thread is wrapped around the needle to create different sizes of knots. This adds additional texture and depth.

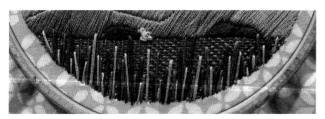

13 **Grass blades.** 3 strands of DMC 3011 + Straight Stitch to add the first layer. 3 strands of DMC 3012 + Straight Stitch to add the second layer. 3 strands of DMC 3348 + Straight Stitch to add the third layer. Stitch at varying lengths. Don't be afraid to have dramatic tall and short stitches in this section. Think wild uncut grass.

14 **Light flowers.** 3 strands of DMC 3823 + Bullion Knot to add blooms to one-third of the taller straight stitches. The length of the bullion knot depends on how many times the thread is wrapped around the needle. These knots use 6–10 thread wraps. 3 strands of DMC 3823 + French Knot to add blooms to one-third of the shorter straight stitches.

15 **Medium flowers.** 3 strands of DMC 745 + Bullion Knot to add blooms to one-third of the taller straight stitches. 3 strands of DMC 745 + French Knot to add blooms to one-third of the shorter straight stitches.

16 **Dark flowers.** 3 strands of DMC 676 + Bullion Knot to add blooms to the last one-third of the taller straight stitches. 3 strands of DMC 676 + French Knot to add blooms to the last one-third of the shorter straight stitches.

17 **To finish your design in the hoop, see page 146.**

Valley Views

SKILL LEVEL: ADVANCED

My husband and I, along with his sister and mom, all drove to the
Grand Canyon one summer. While inside the park, I was struck by the vastness of the
canyon. I would love to go back one day to hike along the bottom and camp inside.

Here's what you'll need to create this design:

- Pattern (page 156)
- 6" (15.2cm) wood embroidery hoop
- Cotton fabric (I used: Speckled in Metallic Teal by Rashida Coleman-Hale for Ruby

Star Society = blue; Metallic Rainbow from JOANN Fabric and Craft = rainbow)
- #5 embroidery needle
- DMC colors: 422, 523, 632, 720, 746, 919, 922, 3011, 3064, 3362,

3363, 3772, 3825, 3826, 3828, 3853, 3856, and 3862
- Scissors
- Erasable pen
- Transfer paper

ILLUSTRATED STITCH GUIDE

This diagram shows what colors and stitches will be used within this design. Please pay special attention to the number key, which will be referenced in the instructions. Follow the instructions for the layer order, details, and tips on each section.

For detailed instructions on how to create each stitch, see the Stitch Glossary starting on page 20.

1 = DMC 632
+ Chain Stitch

2 = DMC 3064
+ Back Stitch

3 = DMC 3362
+ Closed Raised Herringbone Stitch & Stem Stitch

4 = DMC 422
+ Bullion Knot

5 = DMC 523
+ Straight Stitch

6 = DMC 3011
+ Straight Stitch

7 = DMC 3862
+ Satin Stitch

8 = DMC 3772
+ Satin Stitch

9 = DMC 3828
+ Weave Stitch

10 = DMC 3826
+ Back Stitch

11 = DMC 919
+ Long and Short Satin Stitch

12 = DMC 922
+ Satin Stitch

13 = DMC 720
+ Chain Stitch

14 = DMC 3853
+ Satin Stitch

15 = DMC 3825
+ Long and Short Satin Stitch

16 = DMC 3856
+ Satin Stitch

17 = DMC 746
+ Detached Chain Stitch

Contrasting colors are your friend! The blue background makes the orange rock formation look even more impressive.

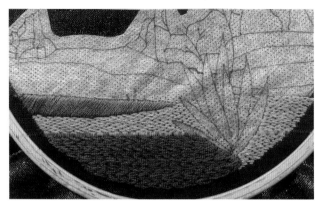

1 **One section labeled 1 in number key.**
4 strands of DMC 632 + Chain Stitch. Stitch in horizontal rows.

2 **Two sections labeled 2 in number key.**
3 strands of DMC 3064 + Back Stitch. Stitch in horizontal rows. Stitch over the smaller plants and around the larger plants.

3 **One section labeled 7 in number key.**
3 strands of DMC 3862 + Satin Stitch. These stitches will be made in an upward diagonal.

4 **One section labeled 3 in number key.**
3 strands of DMC 3362 + Closed Raised Herringbone Stitch to fill in the darker leaves of the yucca plant. 3 strands of DMC 3363 + Closed Raised Herringbone Stitch to fill in the lighter leaves. Because these leaves are so close together, alternate as needed between the dark and light leaves while filling them in.

NOTE: *You can also use the satin stitch to fill in the yucca plant, but I prefer the dimensional effect of the closed raised herringbone stitch.*

5 **Continue section 3.** 3 strands of DMC 3362 + Stem Stitch. Fill in the stalks of the yucca plant.

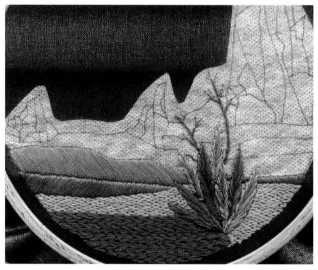

6 **Two sections labeled 8 in number key.**
3 strands of DMC 3772 + Satin Stitch. These stitches should be made at an opposing angle from the layer below it. Stitch around the larger plants.

7 **Determine your method for making the plants.** Because this sits on top of the landscape, you can either eyeball the placement and design from the pattern or use a transfer paper. If using a transfer paper, trace the design onto the paper, then stick it on top of the landscape layers before continuing.

8 **One section labeled 5 in number key.** 3 strands of DMC 523 + Straight Stitch. Each leaf of the plant should be two straight stitches of varying lengths. Start with the leaves in the center of the design and fan out. When stitching leaves into the satin stitch layer, be careful not to split apart the satin stitches and create gaps.

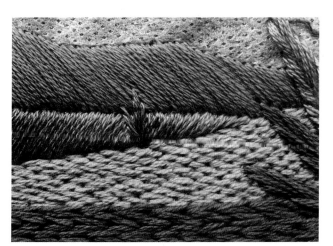

9 **One section labeled 6 in number key.** 2 strands of DMC 3011 + Straight Stitch.

10 **Three sections labeled 9 in number key.** 3 strands of DMC 3828 + Weave Stitch. Create the vertical sections first, then weave in the horizontal rows. Stitch around the larger plants. Because the landscape layer is an uneven shape, some horizontal rows may be longer than others. The closer the stitches, the tighter the weave; the farther spaced out the stitches, the looser the weave, and more fabric will show through.

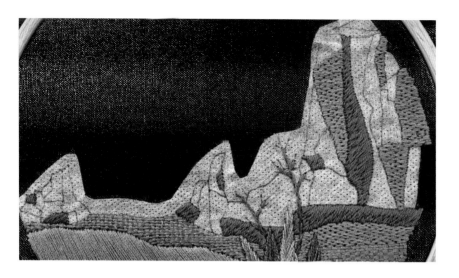

11 Five sections labeled 10 in number key. 3 strands of DMC 3826 + Back Stitch. Stitch in horizontal rows with the rows of stitches offset like bricks. Stitch around the larger plants.

12 Nine sections labeled 11 in number key. 3 strands of DMC 919 + Long and Short Satin Stitch. Stitch at an upward diagonal.

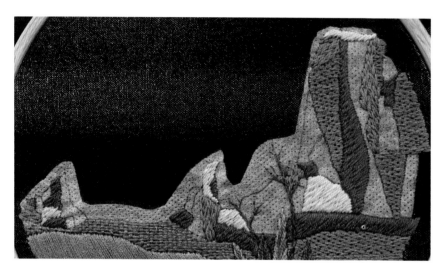

13 Five sections labeled 15 in number key. 3 strands of DMC 3825 + Long and Short Satin Stitch. These stitches follow a similar angle to the previous long and short satin stitch sections.

14 Five sections labeled 13 in number key. 3 strands of DMC 720 + Chain Stitch. Make these stitches in the direction of the longest side of each shape.

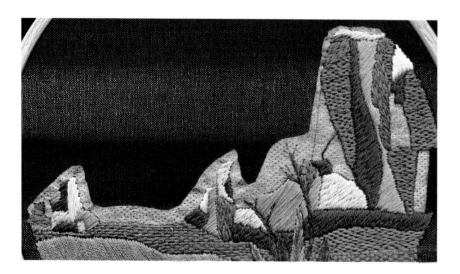

15 Seven sections labeled 12 in number key. 3 strands of DMC 922 + Satin Stitch. Stitch at an upward diagonal.

16 Three sections labeled 16 in number key. 3 strands of 3856 + Satin Stitch. Fill these vertically.

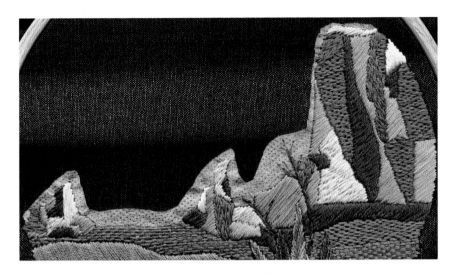

17 **Six sections labeled 14 in number key.** 3 strands of DMC 3853 + Satin Stitch. Fill these horizontally.

18 **One section labeled 17 in number key.** 2 strands of DMC 746 + Detached Chain Stitch. Each flower is made using one detached chain stitch, then filled in using a straight stitch. These flowers should rest on top of the stitches that create the rock face. Be sure not to pull too tightly, otherwise they'll sink and make an indentation in stitches below.

19 **Four sections labeled 4 in number key.** 6 strands of DMC 422 + Bullion Knot. Add rocks to the base of each of the yucca plants with horizontal stitches.

20 **To finish your design in the hoop, see page 146.**

Cenote Plunge

SKILL LEVEL: ADVANCED

Every January, my husband and I take a trip for our anniversary.
One year, we visited Tulum, Mexico, and snorkeled in a cenote (a sinkhole with a pool inside).
I loved how the Tulum cenotes felt like secret swimming places surrounded by plants.

Here's what you'll need to create this design:

- Pattern (page 156)
- 5" (12.7cm) wood embroidery hoop
- Two 7" x 7" (17.8 x 17.8cm) gray tulle
- Cotton fabrics in dark, medium, and light blue (I used Moonscape in Lagoon by Dear Stella, Speckled in Metallic Teal by Rashida Coleman-Hale for Ruby Star Society, and Dash Flow in Twilight by Dear Stella)
- #5 embroidery needle
- DMC colors: 470, 500, 501, 581, 895, 904, 906, 986, 3345, and 3819
- Long sewing pins
- Glue (I used E6000)
- Thick cardstock or thin cardboard
- Scissors
- Erasable pen
- Transfer paper

ILLUSTRATED STITCH GUIDE

This diagram shows what colors and stitches will be used within this design. Follow the instructions for the layer order, details, and tips on each section.

For detailed instructions on how to create each stitch, see the Stitch Glossary starting on page 20.

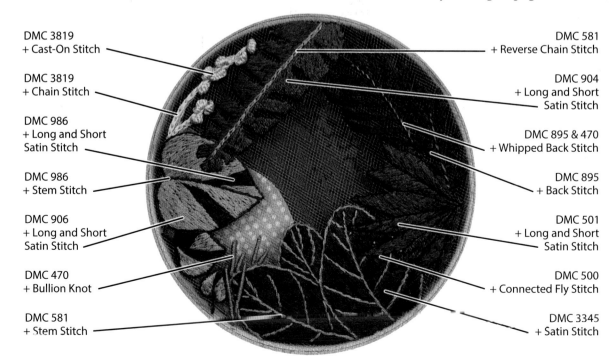

DMC 3819 + Cast-On Stitch

DMC 3819 + Chain Stitch

DMC 986 + Long and Short Satin Stitch

DMC 986 + Stem Stitch

DMC 906 + Long and Short Satin Stitch

DMC 470 + Bullion Knot

DMC 581 + Stem Stitch

DMC 581 + Reverse Chain Stitch

DMC 904 + Long and Short Satin Stitch

DMC 895 & 470 + Whipped Back Stitch

DMC 895 + Back Stitch

DMC 501 + Long and Short Satin Stitch

DMC 500 + Connected Fly Stitch

DMC 3345 + Satin Stitch

This piece layers tulle on top of three blue fabric prints, creating a feast for the eyes.

1 **Trace the outside of the inner hoop onto thick cardstock or thin cardboard.** Cut out the paper circle using paper scissors.

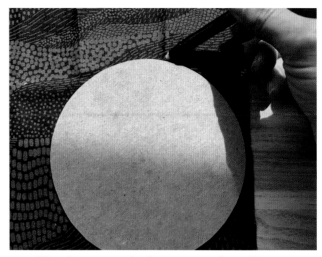

2 **Use the paper circle as a template.** Cut one circle each out of the dark blue, medium blue, and light blue fabrics. Iron fabric is easier to trace and cut.

Tip   If it's hard to see the traced lines on the fabric, flip it over and trace on the back. The back side of most printed cotton fabrics is lighter.

3 **Glue the darkest blue fabric to the circle of card stock using the glue of your choice.**

4 **Cut a curved line about two-thirds of the way down the medium blue fabric.** Glue this fabric on top of the dark blue fabric.

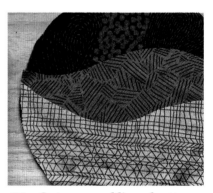

5 **Cut a curved line about halfway down the light blue fabric.** Glue this fabric to the top of the medium blue fabric. Once the glue is dry, trim the fabric to the paper edge of the circle.

6 **Place at least two layers of gray tulle in the embroidery hoop.** Using multiple layers of tulle adds more structure and makes it easier to stitch on. Be gentle when placing the tulle in the hoop and don't pull it too tightly, as it can tear easily. Trace the pattern onto transfer paper. Trim the pattern to the hoop size, peel off the backing, and place it sticky side down onto the tulle. Press gently so as not to tear the tulle.

7 **Ficus leaves.** 3 strands of DMC 3345 + Satin Stitch. Since you're stitching on tulle, you want to hide the tail of the thread underneath the stitches so that it doesn't show through to the front. To do this, create a short horizontal stitch inside the section that will be filled. Then create vertical stitches, from one side of the section to the other, covering the horizontal stitch.

Stitch in sections, working in a zigzag pattern to fill in the leaf. Start in the bottom left, move to the bottom right, stitch the next section on the right, then move to the left, and so on. This keeps the thread within the thread as you stitch and not showing through the tulle. Be sure to stitch around the stem lines of each leaf.

8 **Details on Ficus leaves.** 2 strands of DMC 581 + Stem Stitch. Outline the Ficus leaves and fill in the stem lines. Tuck the tail end of the thread underneath the satin stitch sections to keep the knot from showing through to the front of the fabric when starting the stem stitch. Avoid jumping around on the back whenever possible so the thread doesn't show through. I found it easiest to stitch the center stem line, then the stem lines that branched off it, followed by the leaf outline.

Use short stitches to hug the curves of the leaves. If a single row of the stem stitch doesn't fill in the gap between the satin stitch layers, add in another row next to the first.

9 **Agave plant.** 3 strands of DMC 501 + Long and Short Satin Stitch. Create a horizontal stitch within the shape first, then stitch over it with the long and short satin stitches to hide the tail end. These stitches should be made vertically toward the tip of each leaf.

10 **Ferns.** 3 strands of DMC 895 + Back Stitch. The stem should be made vertically and the leaves horizontally. Stitch the stem line first, then add the leaves to the stem. This allows you to weave the thread on the back along the stem line and jump from leaf to leaf. For each leaf, offset the stitches by stacking the rows like a brick wall.

11 **Fern stems.** 2 strands of DMC 470 + Whipped Back Stitch. Start at one end of the stem line, tucking the knot under previous stitches. Use the eye of the needle to whip the thread around the back stitch. The eye is duller and is less likely to tear the tulle or catch any other threads.

12 **Palm leaf.** 3 strands of DMC 904 + Long and Short Satin Stitch. Stitch diagonally away from the centerline, toward the tip of each leaf section. Create a short horizontal stitch to hide the knot within the section, then stitch over it to fill in the shape.

13 **Palm leaf stem.** 4 strands of DMC 581 + Reverse Chain Stitch.

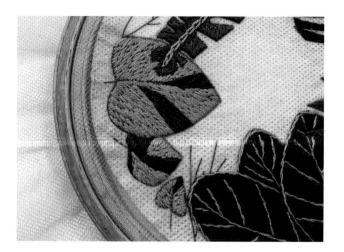

14 **Philodendron leaves.** 3 strands of DMC 906 + Long and Short Satin Stitch to fill in the lighter green portions. Stitch at an outward angle from the stem and around the darker green portions. Tuck the knot like in previous sections. 3 strands of DMC 986 + Long and Short Satin Stitch to fill in the darker green portions. Stitch at an outward angle and tuck the knot.

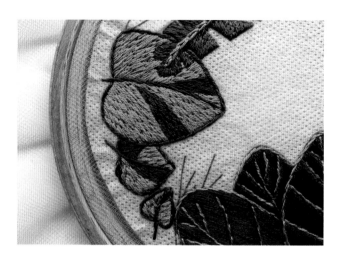

15 **Details on philodendron leaves.** 3 strands of DMC 986 + Stem Stitch. Tuck the knot into the back of the previous stitches of the leaf. Create the centerline, followed by the outer edge. Make short stitches so that the stem stitch hugs the curves of the leaf shape.

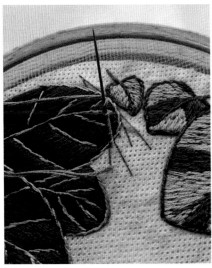  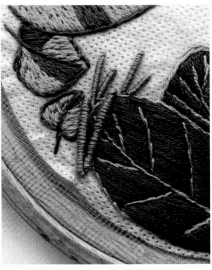

16 **Bottom-left foliage.** 6 strands of DMC 470 + Bullion Knot. Start with the shorter foliage, and tuck the end knot into the back of the Ficus leaves. Instead of sliding the needle in and out of the fabric, push the needle through the end of the bullion knot and then leave it sticking up at the other side to wrap the thread around the needle. This way, the needle is less likely to get caught on the tulle and it's easier to stitch the longer bullion knots. After stitching, follow the line of the bullion knot and bring the thread down into the back of the Ficus leaves to hide it on the back.

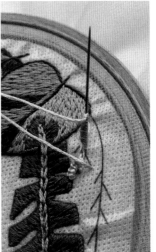 

17 **Top-left foliage stems.** 4 strands of DMC 3819 + Chain Stitch. Tuck the knot into the back of the philodendron leaf. Then use the chain stitch to create the stem line from the base of the philodendron to the top of the foliage.

18 **Top-left foliage leaves.** 4 strands of DMC 3819 + Cast-On Stitch. Add leaves to the stem line as you work your way back down the foliage. Start each cast-on stitch at the base of the stem line. Like the bullion knots, do not slide the needle through the fabric; instead, bring the needle down and then partially back up through the other end of the cast-on stitch.

19 **Details on agave plant.** 1 strand of DMC 500 + Connected Fly Stitch. Outlining is an easy way to define a shape, clean up any uneven edges, and add extra details. Make short stitches while outlining the agave leaves to hug their curves.

20 **Wash away the stabilizer pattern prior to adding the backing.**

21 **To finish your design in the hoop, see page 146.** Before continuing with step 3 of those instructions, place the watery backing against the back of the embroidery.

Flower Field Mountains

SKILL LEVEL: ADVANCED

Summer is undoubtedly the best time to visit the Seattle area.
We have gorgeous weather, there are many amazing hikes, and the landscape is awash
with colors and greenery. This project is inspired by that Seattle summer feeling.

Here's what you'll need to create this design:

- Pattern (page 157)
- 5" (12.7cm) wood embroidery hoop
- Cotton fabric (I used: Speckled in Metallic Teal by Rashida Coleman-Hale for Ruby Star
- Society = blue; Quarry Trail in Mango by Anna Graham for Robert Kaufman = pink)
- #5 embroidery needle
- DMC colors: 18, 26, 159, 452, 471, 505, 581, 731, 733, 832, 966, 3341, 3779, and 3833
- Scissors
- Pencil or erasable pen
- Transfer paper (optional)

ILLUSTRATED STITCH GUIDE

This diagram shows what colors and stitches will be used within this design. Follow the instructions for the layer order, details, and tips on each section.

For detailed instructions on how to create each stitch, see the Stitch Glossary starting on page 20.

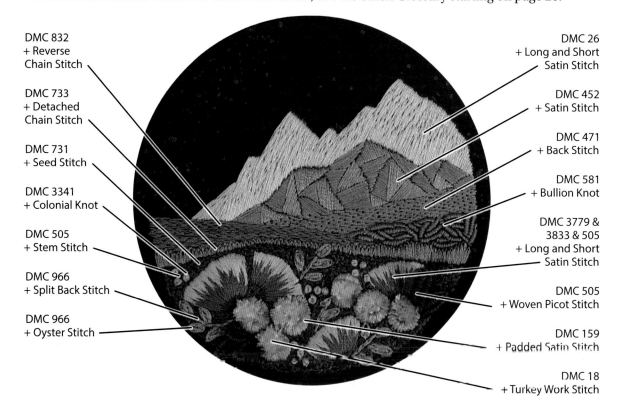

DMC 832 + Reverse Chain Stitch

DMC 733 + Detached Chain Stitch

DMC 731 + Seed Stitch

DMC 3341 + Colonial Knot

DMC 505 + Stem Stitch

DMC 966 + Split Back Stitch

DMC 966 + Oyster Stitch

DMC 26 + Long and Short Satin Stitch

DMC 452 + Satin Stitch

DMC 471 + Back Stitch

DMC 581 + Bullion Knot

DMC 3779 & 3833 & 505 + Long and Short Satin Stitch

DMC 505 + Woven Picot Stitch

DMC 159 + Padded Satin Stitch

DMC 18 + Turkey Work Stitch

The pink and yellow flowers pop against a dark background, but using pink fabric balances the pinks in the piece. There are so many possibilities!

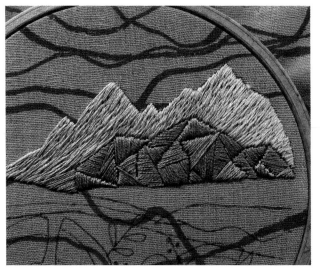

1 **Top mountains.** 3 strands of DMC 26 + Long and Short Satin Stitch. Create these stitches on an angle to easily fill in the peaks and angles of the mountain range lines.

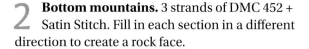

2 **Bottom mountains.** 3 strands of DMC 452 + Satin Stitch. Fill in each section in a different direction to create a rock face.

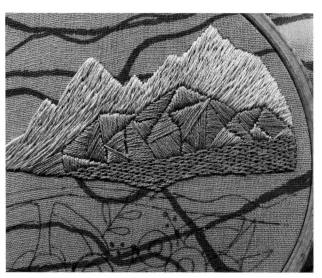

3 **Top-right landscape.** 3 strands of DMC 471 + Back Stitch. Make these stitches in horizontal rows. Offset each row like bricks.

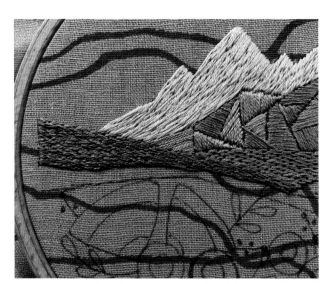

4 **Top-left landscape.** 3 strands of DMC 832 + Reverse Chain Stitch. Make these stitches in horizontal rows.

5 **Middle landscape.** 3 strands of DMC 733 + Detached Chain Stitch. Make these stitches vertically so they're parallel to one another. Each stitch will be the height of this section, meaning some stitches will be shorter or taller than others.

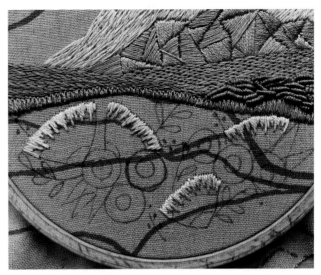

6 **Middle-right landscape.** 6 strands of DMC 581 + Bullion Knot. Make these stitches in any direction to fill the space. It's best to stitch the areas around this section first because these stitches sit higher off the fabric.

7 **Tops of thistle flower petals.** 3 strands of DMC 3779 + Long and Short Satin Stitch. The pattern line is a general guide and stitches will be longer or shorter than the guideline. Use dramatic lengths of stitches so that when the next row is blended into this one it will look purposeful and less like an uneven line.

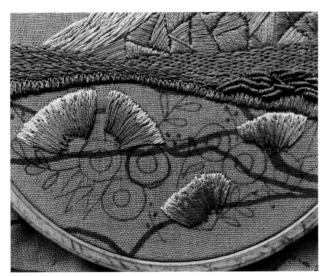

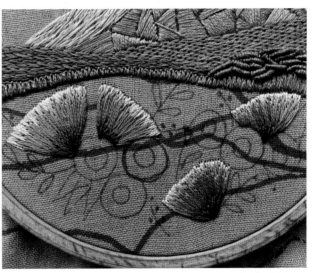

8 **Bottoms of thistle flower petals.** 3 strands of DMC 3833 + Long and Short Satin Stitch. Overlap some of these stitches. Because these flowers are triangular, shorter stitches may be overlapped by longer stitches to radially fill in this section.

9 **Bases of thistle flowers.** 3 strands of DMC 505 + Long and Short Satin Stitch. Shorter stitches may be overlapped by longer stitches to radially fill in this section.

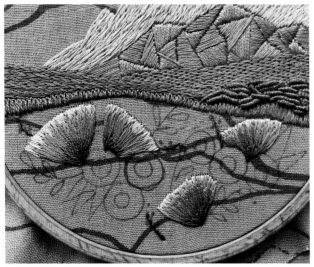

10 **Dot flower stems.** 3 strands of DMC 505 + Stem Stitch.

11 **3D leaves.** 6 strands of DMC 505 + Woven Picot Stitch. Start with the leaves furthest forward on the design. Be careful not to catch the working thread on the woven picot leaves. Pin them out of the way as you stitch the leaves below them.

12 **Foliage.** 3 strands of DMC 966 + Split Back Stitch for stems. 6 strands of DMC 966 + Oyster Stitch for leaves. Each leaf is one oyster stitch.

13 **Aster petals.** 3 strands of DMC 159 + Padded Satin Stitch. For the padding, I used a chain stitch on the inside of the outer ring and a back stitch on the inside of the inner ring. You can use whatever stitches you'd like for padding.

14 **Aster centers.** 6 strands of DMC 18 + Turkey Work. After the sections are filled with turkey work, trim them to size. Make the turkey work longer than you'd like it so that you can trim it down afterwards; it's easier to start longer then trim shorter.

15 **Dot flowers.** 4 strands of DMC 3341 + Colonial Knot. Each knot will be an orange bud on the stems.

16 **Bottom landscape.** 6 strands of DMC 731 + Seed Stitch. These stitches should densely fill the section around the flowers and leaves.

17 **To finish your design in the hoop, see page 146.**

Forest Foraging

SKILL LEVEL: ADVANCED

I will admit, I have never been mushroom foraging.
But I was surprised to see the variety of mushrooms that grow around
my neighborhood. Maybe I'll give it a try one day!

Here's what you'll need to create this design:

- Pattern (page 157)
- 8" (20.3cm) triangle wood embroidery hoop
- 10" x 10" (25.4 x 25.4cm) fabric (I used Moda Marbles in Dusty Purple by Moda Fabrics)
- Seven 10" x 10" (25.4 x 25.4cm) gray tulle
- #5 embroidery needle
- DMC colors: 152, 316, 355, 422, 433, 469, 471, 543, 580, 677, 731, 898, 935, 951, 3011, 3012, 3031, 3051, 3371, 3777, 3821, and 3830
- Scissors
- Erasable pen
- Transfer paper

ILLUSTRATED STITCH GUIDE

This diagram shows what colors and stitches will be used within this design. Follow the instructions for the layer order, details, and tips on each section.

For detailed instructions on how to create each stitch, see the Stitch Glossary starting on page 20.

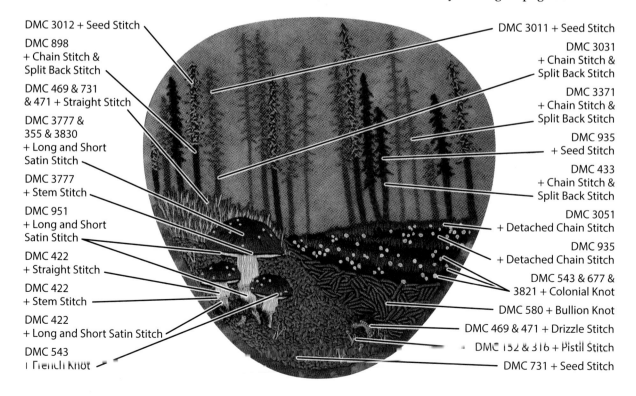

DMC 3012 + Seed Stitch

DMC 898 + Chain Stitch & Split Back Stitch

DMC 469 & 731 & 471 + Straight Stitch

DMC 3777 & 355 & 3830 + Long and Short Satin Stitch

DMC 3777 + Stem Stitch

DMC 951 + Long and Short Satin Stitch

DMC 422 + Straight Stitch

DMC 422 + Stem Stitch

DMC 422 + Long and Short Satin Stitch

DMC 543 + French Knot

DMC 3011 + Seed Stitch

DMC 3031 + Chain Stitch & Split Back Stitch

DMC 3371 + Chain Stitch & Split Back Stitch

DMC 935 + Seed Stitch

DMC 433 + Chain Stitch & Split Back Stitch

DMC 3051 + Detached Chain Stitch

DMC 935 + Detached Chain Stitch

DMC 543 & 677 & 3821 + Colonial Knot

DMC 580 + Bullion Knot

DMC 469 & 471 + Drizzle Stitch

DMC 152 & 316 + Pistil Stitch

DMC 731 + Seed Stitch

Layering tulle over part of the background fabric can transform the color while adding depth to the design.

1 **Place the fabric in the hoop and trace the pattern.** Don't worry about the mushrooms—you'll add those in later. Pin two layers of gray tulle on top of the fabric in the embroidery hoop. Make sure the fabric is flat while placing it on top of the hoop and that the bottom edge of the tulle overlaps the top of the landscape layers. You'll be stacking tulle layers throughout to create depth with this design.

2 **First layer of trees.** 3 strands of DMC 3371 + Chain Stitch to make the trunks. Stitch these trees in a single chain stitch row vertically. Stitch from the top of the tree to the bottom of the drawn landscape layers. 3 strands of DMC 3371 + Split Back Stitch to add branches to the trees.

3 **Pin two more layers of gray tulle to the front of the embroidery hoop.** Ensure the bottom edges are aligned and overlap the top of the drawn landscape layers.

4 **Second layer of trees.** 3 strands of DMC 3031 + Chain Stitch to make the trunks. Create these trees using two vertical rows. 3 strands of DMC 3031 + Split Back Stitch to add branches to the trees. 3 strands of DMC 3011 + Seed Stitch to add foliage. These stitches should overlap and be sporadically stitched along the tree branches and trunks.

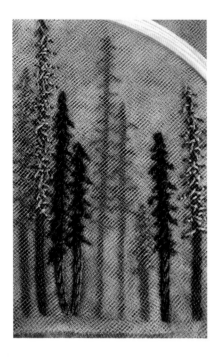

5 **Pin another two layers of tulle to the top of the embroidery hoop.** Ensure the bottom edges are aligned and overlap the top of the drawn landscape layers.

6 **Third layer of trees.** 3 strands of DMC 898 + Chain Stitch to make the trunks. Create these trees using two vertical rows. 3 strands of DMC 898 + Split Back Stitch to add branches to the trees.

7 **Pin another layer of gray tulle on top of the fabric.** Ensure the bottom edges are aligned and overlap the top of the drawn landscape layers.

8 **Fourth layer of trees.** 3 strands of DMC 433 + Chain Stitch to make the trunks. Create these trees using two vertical rows. 3 strands of DMC 433 + Split Back Stitch to add branches to the trees.

9 **Unscrew the embroidery hoop.** Trim the layers of tulle that overlap the top of the landscape layers so that there is only a ¼" (6mm) overlap. Tighten the hoop again ensuring all layers of tulle and fabric are inside the hoop. Make sure the tulle is flat when tightening the hoop and don't tug along the edges or it will tear.

10 **Top-right landscape.** 4 strands of DMC 3051 + Detached Chain Stitch to fill in the top row of the section. Fill in with each stitch made vertically. Cover the tulle that overlaps this section with this row of stitches. 4 strands of DMC 935 + Detached Chain Stitch to fill in the second row. Slightly overlap the last row, covering up the bottoms of the stitches. Continue alternating between colors in each row of this section until all rows are filled.

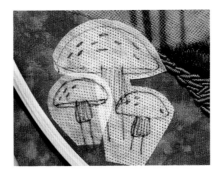

11 **Middle-right landscape.** 6 strands of DMC 580 + Bullion Knot. The bullion knots should vary in length and direction.

12 **Trace the mushroom design onto a transfer paper.** Peel off the back and place the pattern sticky side down onto the fabric. I used a transfer paper because the mushroom caps overlap the top of the tulle and make it hard to trace the design on top.

13 **Mushroom caps.** 3 strands of DMC 3777 + Long and Short Satin Stitch to fill in the top third of the mushroom cap. Because the mushroom cap is rounded, the stitches toward the top of the cap will overlap, like the radial satin stitch. 3 strands of DMC 355 + Long and Short Satin Stitch to fill in the next third of the cap. 3 strands of DMC 3830 + Long and Short Satin Stitch to fill in the last third of the cap.

14 **Underside of mushroom caps.** 3 strands of DMC 951 + Long and Short Satin Stitch. Make these stitches horizontally.

15 **Top of mushroom stems.** DMC 951 + Long and Short Satin Stitch. Make these stitches vertically.

16 **Middle of mushroom stems.** 2 strands of DMC 422 + Long and Short Satin Stitch. Make these stitches vertically.

17 **Details on top of mushroom stems.** 2 strands of DMC 422 + Straight Stitch. Add lines on top of the mushroom stem to create depth.

18 **Details on middle of mushroom stems.** 2 strands of DMC 422 + Stem Stitch. Create a line along the bottom of the wider part of the top mushroom stem.

19 **Bottom of mushroom stems.** 2 strands of DMC 951 + Long and Short Satin Stitch.

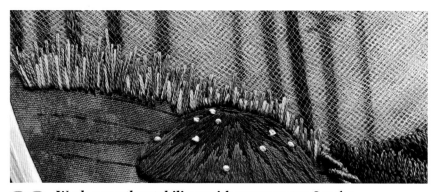

20 **Mushroom cap edges.** 2 strands of DMC 3777 + Stem Stitch. Outline the cream underside of the mushroom cap. Because this shape is curved, make the stem stitches a little shorter so that the stitches hug the curves of the shape.

21 **Spots on mushroom caps.** 2 strands of DMC 543 + French Knot. Add as many or as few as you'd like!

22 **Wash away the stabilizer with warm water.** Let the embroidery dry.

23 **Top-left landscape.** 3 strands of DMC 469 + Straight Stitch to add the first layer of grass. These lines will be spaced out within the first row and vary in length. 3 strands of DMC 731 + Straight Stitch to add another layer of straight stitches in the same section. 3 strands of DMC 471 + Straight Stitch to add a third layer of straight stitches. This third layer should fill in the last gaps in the top row.

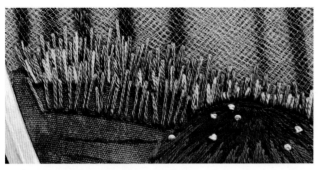

24 **Repeat step 23 on the next row to continue filling in this landscape layer.** Each row of stitches will vary in length to create the look of overgrown grass.

25 **Bottom landscape.** 6 strands of DMC 731 + Seed Stitch. These stitches should overlap to create a thick texture.

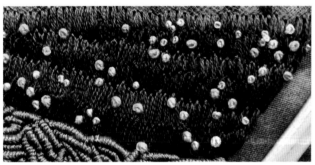

26 **Flowers on top-right landscape.** 4 strands of DMC 3821 + Colonial Knot to add the darkest color dots. 3 strands of DMC 677 + Colonial Knot to add medium dots. 2 strands of DMC 543 + Colonial Knot to add the lightest dots. These dots will look like distant flowers.

27 **3D leaves.** 6 strands of DMC 469 + Drizzle Stitch to create darker leaves. 6 strands of DMC 471 + Drizzle Stitch to create lighter leaves. Stitch leaves by the base of the mushrooms and to the right of the mushroom section.

28 **Flowers on bottom landscape.** 2 strands of DMC 152 + Pistil Stitch to create lighter flowers. 2 strands of DMC 316 + Pistil Stitch to create darker flowers.

29 **To finish your design in the hoop, see** **page 146.**

How to Finish the Embroidery in the Hoop

One of the ways I like to finish an embroidery is in the hoop with a closed back and a sawtooth hook. This makes it easy to hang the embroidery like a picture frame. Finishing the back of a hoop is optional and you can choose to finish your embroidery however you like.

You'll need:

- Finished embroidery project
- #5 embroidery needle
- Thread
- Scissors
- Felt piece (larger than hoop)
- Sawtooth hook
- Long sewing pins

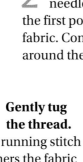

1 **Trim the fabric to about 1" (2.5cm) from hoop edge.** Measure a length of thread that is longer than the circumference of the hoop and thread the needle.

2 **Use the running stitch to stitch around the fabric.** Bring the needle up through the fabric and back down a short distance from the first point. Leave a space, then bring the needle back up through the fabric. Continue this until the running stitch has been made all the way around the back of the hoop.

3 **Gently tug the thread.** The running stitch gathers the fabric tightly on the back side of the hoop. Knot the thread.

4 **Lay your hoop on a piece of felt.** Keep the fabric gathered around the back of the hoop. Trace the hoop circumference on felt.

5 **Cut the felt to size of your hoop.** Trim the felt so it is slightly smaller than the circumference of the embroidery hoop. This will ensure the felt doesn't protrude from the back.

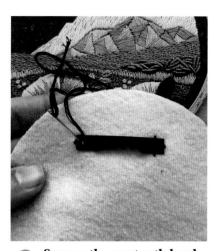

6 **Sew on the sawtooth hook 1" (2.5cm) from the top of the felt circle.** Use 6 strands of embroidery thread. Now is a great time to add any additional stitching to the back, such as a date, your initials, or a label.

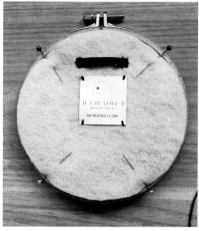

7 **Pin the felt backing to the gathered fabric at the back of the hoop.** Align the sawtooth hook with the screw at the top of the embroidery hoop.

8 **Use the whip stitch to attach the felt to back of hoop.** Bring the needle through the underside of the felt, in between where the felt and fabric will meet.

9 **Bring the needle through the fabric on the back of the embroidery, then through the felt.** Tug the thread gently so that the thread whips around the two pieces.

10 **Continue stitching around the hoop.** Remove the pins when stitching. Knot the thread at the end.

Patterns

You can download the pattern files shown on pages 148–157 at foxpatterns.com/how-to-embroider-texture-and-pattern.

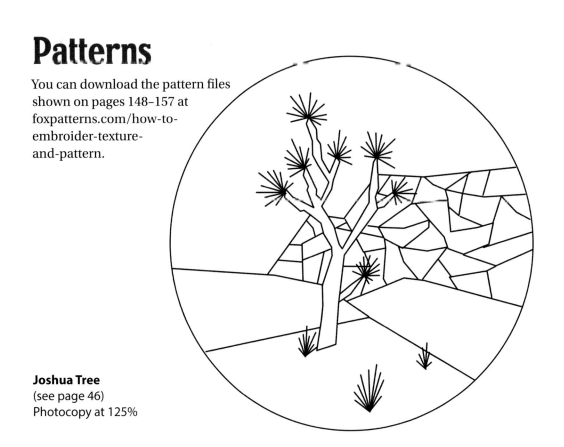

Joshua Tree
(see page 46)
Photocopy at 125%

Where the Forest Meets the Beach
(see page 50)
Photocopy at 100%

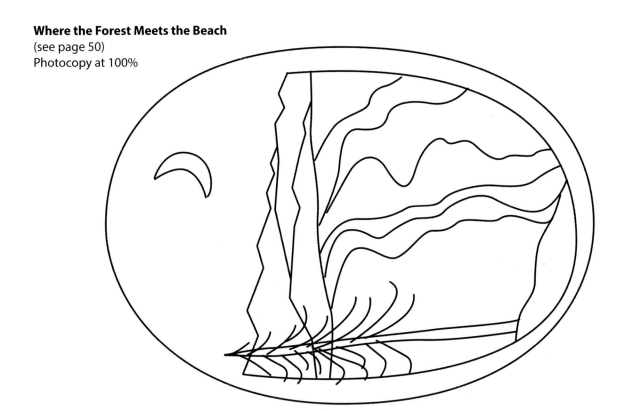

Mojave Hues
(see page 54)
Photocopy at 150%

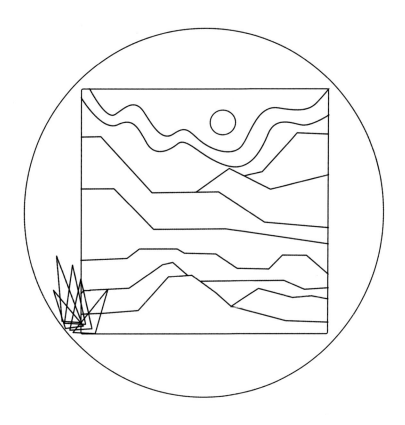

Hidden Beach Cove
(see page 60)
Photocopy at 100%

Mountains at Sunset
(see page 64)
Photocopy at 125%

Desert Arches
(see page 68)
Photocopy at 125%

Purple Mountains Majesty
(see page 72)
Photocopy at 100%

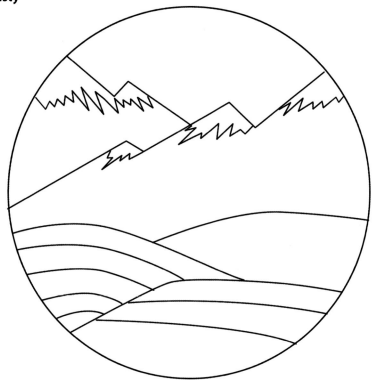

A Walk Among the Wildflowers
(see page 76)
Photocopy at 100%

Scenic Lookout
(see page 82)
Photocopy at 125%

Desert Oasis
(see page 88)
Photocopy at 125%

A Pacific Northwest Spring
(see page 92)
Photocopy at 125%

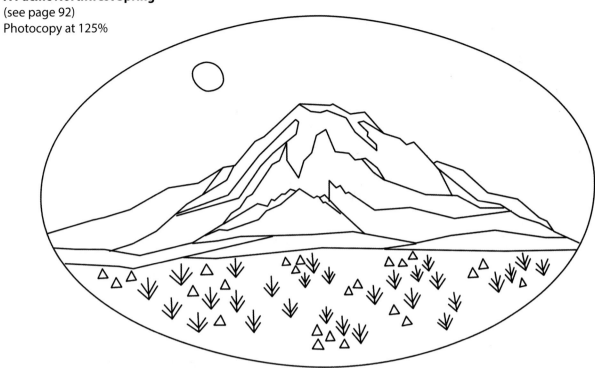

Mountain Brook
(see page 96)
Photocopy at 150%

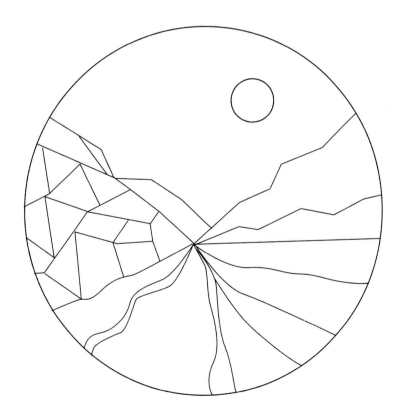

From the Heartland
(see page 100)
Photocopy at 167%

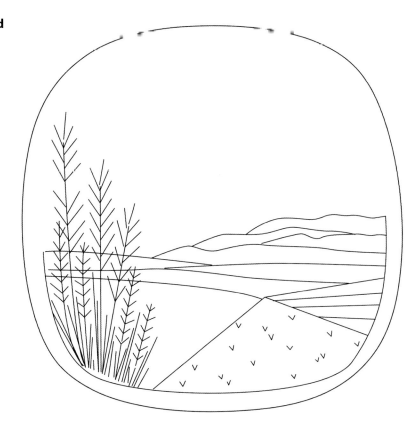

It Was All a Mirage
(see page 106)
Photocopy at 150%

Tropical Waterfall
(see page 110)
Photocopy at 125%

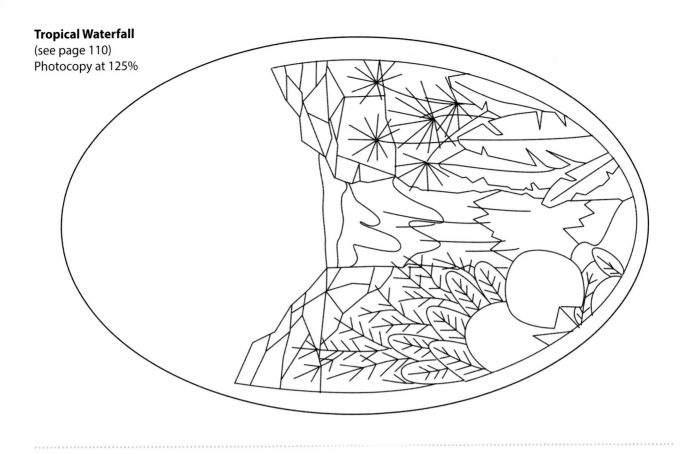

A Walk Along the English Seaside
(see page 116)
Photocopy at 125%

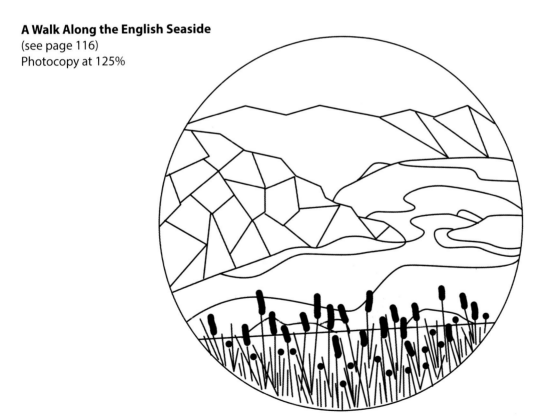

Valley Views
(see page 120)
Photocopy at 150%

Cenote Plunge
(see page 126)
Photocopy at 125%

Flower Field Mountains
(see page 134)
Photocopy at 125%

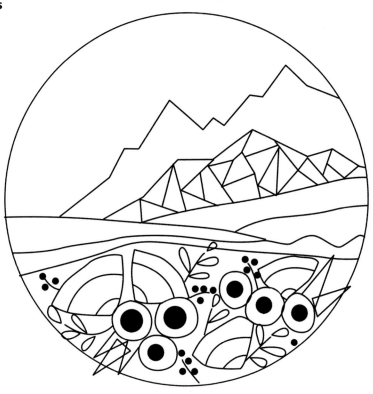

Forest Foraging
(see page 140)
Photocopy at 200%

About Melissa

Melissa Galbraith is the fiber artist behind MCreativeJ. She was born and raised in the desert of Washington state, where her mother instilled a love of making things by hand at an early age. Drawing on her love of nature, Melissa creates whimsical and modern embroidery patterns and kits. She loves making the art of hand embroidery easy and approachable with her embroidery kits, patterns, and workshops.

Melissa was reintroduced to hand embroidery after finding her desk job to be monotonous and needing a creative outlet. She loves that embroidery allows her to play with texture and color and that it's a portable craft. Along the way, Melissa found that many craft-minded makers also wanted to learn how to embroider but were daunted by where to start. Thanks to this and a love of teaching, Melissa began to share her embroidery knowledge.

Melissa's embroidery kits and patterns make it easy to learn a new craft for makers of all skill levels. She enjoys seeing makers fall in love with the needle arts, especially that magical "ah-ha" moment of learning something new.

Index

Note: Page numbers in *italics* indicate projects/patterns (pattern page numbers are in parentheses).

B
back stitch, 20
  split back stitch, 38
  whipped back stitch, 42–43
bullion knot, 21
buttonhole stitch, detached, 26–27

C
cast-on stitch, 21–22
Cenote Plunge, *126–33 (156)*
chain stitch, 23
  detached chain stitch/lazy daisy, 27
  reverse chain stitch, 35–36
closed fly stitch, 28–29
closed raised herringbone stitch, 23–24
colonial knot, 24–25
connected fly stitch, 29–30
couching stitch, 25
cutting thread, 13

D
Danish knot, 26
Desert Arches, *68–71 (150)*
Desert Oasis, *88–91 (152)*
detached buttonhole stitch, 26–27
detached chain stitch/lazy daisy, 27
drizzle stitch, 28

F
fabric, 8
finishing embroidery in hoop, 146–47
Flower Field Mountains, *134–39 (157)*
fly stitch (closed, connected), 28–30
Forest Foraging, *140–45 (157)*
French knot, 30–31
From the Heartland, *100–105 (154)*

G
granitos stitch, 31

H
herringbone stitch, closed raised, 23–24
Hidden Beach Cove, *60–63 (149)*
hoops
  about, 9
  finishing embroidery in, 146–47
  placing fabric in, 10

I
It Was All a Mirage, *106–9 (154)*

J
Joshua Tree, *46–49 (148)*

K
knots. *See* stitches
knotting thread, 17–19

L
lazy daisy/detached chain stitch, 27
light box/window, 11
long and short satin stitch, 31–32

M
materials, 8–19
  choosing thread and fabric, 8
  exploring color and pattern, 8
  fabric, 8
  knotting thread, 17–19
  needles, 15–16
  scissors, 15
  thread prep, 13–14
Mojave Hues, *54–59 (149)*
Mountain Brook, *96–99 (153)*
Mountains at Sunset, *64–67 (150)*

N
needles
  about: to use, 15
  threading, 16

O
oyster stitch, 32–33

P
Pacific Northwest Spring, *92–95 (153)*
padded satin stitch, 34
patterns, 148–57. *See also* projects
  about: overview of, 6
  transferring, 11–12
picot stitch, woven, 43–44
pistil stitch, 34
projects, overview of patterns/designs, 6, 45
projects: advanced
  Cenote Plunge, *126–33 (156)*
  Flower Field Mountains, *134–39 (157)*
  Forest Foraging, *140–45 (157)*
  It Was All a Mirage, *106–9 (154)*
  Tropical Waterfall, 110–15 (155)
  Valley Views, *120–25 (156)*
  A Walk Along the English Seaside, *116–19 (155)*
projects: beginner
  Desert Arches, *68–71 (150)*
  Hidden Beach Cove, *60–63 (149)*
  Joshua Tree, *46–49 (148)*
  Mojave Hues, *54–59 (149)*
  Mountains at Sunset, *64–67 (150)*
  Purple Mountains Majesty, *72–75 (151)*
  Where the Forest Meets the Beach, *50–53 (148)*
projects: intermediate
  Desert Oasis, *88–91 (152)*
  From the Heartland, *100–105 (154)*
  Mountain Brook, *96–99 (153)*
  A Pacific Northwest Spring, *92–95 (153)*
  Scenic Outlook, *82–87 (152)*
  A Walk Among the Wildflowers, *76–81 (151)*
Purple Mountains Majesty, *72–75 (151)*

Index

R
radial satin stitch, 35
reverse chain stitch, 35–36
running stitch, 36

S
satin stitch, 37
   long and short, 31–32
   padded, 34
   radial, 35
Scenic Outlook, *82–87 (152)*
scissors, 15
seed stitch, 37
short and long satin stitch, 31–32
split back stitch, 38
splitting thread, 14
stem stitch, 38
stitches. *See also* satin stitch
   back stitch, 20
   bullion knot, 21
   cast-on stitch, 21–22
   chain stitch, 23
   closed raised herringbone stitch,
      23–24
   colonial knot, 24–25
   couching stitch, 25
   Danish knot, 26
   detached buttonhole stitch,
      26–27
   detached chain stitch/lazy daisy,
      27
   drizzle stitch, 28
   fly stitch (closed, connected),
      28–30
   French knot, 30–31
   granitos stitch, 31
   oyster stitch, 32–33
   pistil stitch, 34
   reverse chain stitch, 35–36
   running stitch, 36
   seed stitch, 37
   split back stitch, 38
   stem stitch, 38
   straight stitch, 39
   tulip stitch, 39–40
   turkey work stitch, 40
   weave stitch/woven stitch, 41
   wheatear stitch, 42
   whipped back stitch, 42–43
   woven picot stitch, 43–44
straight stitch, 39

T
thread
   6-strand, to use, 13
   cutting, 13
   knotting, 17–19
   splitting, 14
threading needles, 16
transfer paper, 12
transferring pattern, 11–12
Tropical Waterfall, *110–15 (155)*
tulip stitch, 39–40
turkey work stitch, 40

V
Valley Views, *120–25 (156)*

W
A Walk Along the English Seaside,
   116–19 (155)
A Walk Among the Wildflowers,
   76–81 (151)
weave stitch, 41
wheatear stitch, 42
Where the Forest Meets the Beach,
   50–53 (148)
whipped back stitch, 42–43
woven picot stitch, 43–44
woven stitch, 41